JOINING
JESUS
ON HIS MISSION

Greg Finke has modeled rare courage on his own life journey. Now you can benefit. Don't hesitate to learn from the practical experience and true grit of this missional pioneer!

—Will Mancini, Founder of Auxano; author of *Church Unique*

Whenever people invite me onto a journey, I want to know if they are familiar with where we are going. Greg Finke knows the lay of the land in terms of moving into missionary mode as a Jesus-follower. When he talks about joining the mission of Jesus, he's done it. Because of that, his is a trusted trail guide's voice. Listen to him. Better yet, join him!

— Reggie McNeal, best-selling author of *The Present Future* and *Missional Renaissance*

Greg Finke gets it. If you're going to lead people — lots of people — to follow Jesus, you need a method that is simple but powerful, true to God's Word but translated into the vernacular. That's the power behind Greg's ministry and the power behind this book.

— Bill Woolsey, Senior Pastor, CrossPoint Community Church; Founding Leader, FiveTwo Network

I have the highest regard for Greg Finke and his book *Joining Jesus on His Mission*. In it he has provided clear, simple, and highly effective practices that guide us as we seek to learn to live missionally. I highly commend his work to you.

—Jim Herrington, Founding Director, Mission Houston; Team Leader, Faithwalking; author of *The Leader's Journey*

This book is incredible! Greg's revelation on reaching the world for Christ is refreshing, relieving and invigorating. He shows us how to follow Jesus and get beyond all the thinking that can paralyze us and suck the joy out of our calling.

—Sarah Guldalian, Producer of Evangelism Training, Lutheran Hour Ministries

If I were to recommend one book that invites people into the mission of God, this would be it! Practical! Playful! Powerful! Greg is a master at helping people simply start!

—Dr. Jock Ficken, Executive Leader, Pastoral Leadership Institute

Wherever I travel in America I find Christians and their churches in desperate need of a reliable "road map" to help them navigate our post-churched terrain. *Joining Jesus on His Mission* hits the mark. A must read for mission minded Christians!

—Dr. Robert Newton, President, California-Nevada-Hawaii District, LCMS

Adventure! Most people love a good one. But, truth be told, they would rather watch it in the comfort of their own living room than actually experience it in real life. Good news! Greg Finke demonstrates how anyone, no matter how unadventuresome, can join Jesus on the most exciting mission field in the world. And we don't even have to leave our own neighborhood to do it!

—Dr. Terry Tieman, Executive Director, Transforming Churches Network

Greg hits it out of the park with *Joining Jesus on His Mission*. This book is not about understanding the theory of missions. It is a launching pad for you to actually join Jesus on His mission.

—Rev. Gary Faith, Executive for Parish Ministries, Southern District, LCMS

With all the approaches for neighborhood ministry available today the simple barometer for me is this: would I actually use this in my neighborhood? After all, I have to live with these people! Greg Finke's approach is one I can use in my neighborhood. He has developed a missional tool that works in the culture in which I live.

—Dr. John Denninger, President, Southeastern District, LCMS

Greg has a wonderful way of taking the fear and apprehension out of missional living. He has simplified what seems complex and, with his engaging style, quickly invites readers to say, "I can do this!" With real life examples and solid Biblical theology this is an excellent contribution from a missional practitioner and leader and a powerful teaching tool for those involved in missional communities.

—Dr. Peter Meier, Executive Director, Center for United States Missions

Joining Jesus on His Mission is excellent. Simple, powerful, practical, applicable. This is a great tool for helping believers join Jesus on His mission. I had several Kairos moments as I read. Greg's insights alter the way we see mission.

—Al Doering, Senior Pastor, Houston; 3DM Frontier Leader

What Greg has brought together in these pages is an intensely practical and deeply passionate exploration of what it means to join Jesus in his work of loving and saving the world. For those looking to saturate their day-to-day life with mission and meaning *Joining Jesus* is essential reading.

—Matt Popovits, Pastor/Planter, Our Saviour, New York City

JOINING
JESUS
ON HIS MISSION

How to Be an
Everyday Missionary

TENTH
POWER

ELGIN, IL · TYLER, TX

TENTHPOWERPUBLISHING

www.tenthpowerpublishing.com

Design by Inkwell Creative

Softcover ISBN 978-1-938840-02-9

e-book ISBN 978-1-938840-03-6

10 9 8 7 6 5

This book is dedicated to our neighbors in Westover Park

and especially the friends in our missional communities.

You have taught us what is written here!

TABLE OF CONTENTS

Foreword..13

Introduction..15

Chapter 1: What's Jesus Up To?..19

Chapter 2: Joining Jesus...27

Chapter 3: The River Moved..37

Chapter 4: Are You Stalling?...45

Chapter 5: Could It Be This Simple?................................51

Chapter 6: An Inefficiently Effective Strategy................57

Chapter 7: Seeking What's Already Happening...............67

Chapter 8: The Kingdom of God.......................................73

Chapter 9: What Does the Kingdom of God
                    Look Like?...83

Chapter 10: The Mission of God.......................................91

Chapter 11: Getting into Position Every Day.................97

Chapter 12: Seeking the Kingdom.................................103

Chapter 13: Hearing from Jesus....................................107

Chapter 14: Talking with People....................................111

Chapter 15: Doing Good..119

Chapter 16: Ministering through Prayer.......................125

Chapter 17: The Missional Party.....................................135

Chapter 18: What Will Your Story Be?...........................147

Chapter 19: With a Little Help from My Friends...........153

Benediction...167

Discussion Guide...169

Appendix 1: Frequently Asked Questions.....................181

Appendix 2: Neighborhood Prayer Map........................190

FOREWORD

In John 3, Nicodemus, the professional teacher of religion, comes to Jesus to get remedial instruction on the kingdom of God, how it works, how to see it, and how to participate in it. Jesus says to Nicodemus, "You're the teacher of Israel and do not understand these things?" I'll be honest, as a professor at a seminary I had several Nicodemus moments when reading this book. It's no run of the mill book on evangelism, missional communities, or missional living. Instead, it's like sitting at Jesus' feet and having a conversation about how the kingdom of God is actually at work in everyday life. Whether you're a seminary prof, student, mature member of a missional community, life-long churchgoer, or brand new Jesus follower, the Lord Jesus will meet you in this book and invite you into the work He's already doing.

Most books on evangelism are high on demands and low on practical ideas for implementation. *Joining Jesus on His Mission* is just the opposite. It's practical enough for anyone to understand but full of great, Gospel-packed theology. It approaches mission and evangelism from the reality that in Jesus, the Kingdom of God is already at work in our world today. God has taken responsibility for saving the world by Christ's crucifixion and resurrection and by sending the Spirit. Jesus is still very much on His mission to redeem the world to Himself. So, no need for demanding and shaming Christians into evangelism. As Finke elegantly puts it, "We're not on mission *for* Jesus but *with* Jesus!"

I plan on reading this book again, this time with my wife, then with my students, then with my pastor and church. This afternoon I was at a family gathering, and I immediately put some of this book to work. I opened my eyes to look where Jesus might be ready to harvest and was surprised to see the living and active Kingdom of God at work at a family gathering! The best recommendation I can give for this book, though, is that Finke is actually living this stuff. Thanks, Greg, for keeping our eyes on Jesus through your words and through your life!

—Ben Haupt, Assistant Professor of Practical Theology, Concordia Seminary, St. Louis

INTRODUCTION

Recently we spent a few days with our friends in the Nantahala National Forest in the mountains of North Carolina. One of the highlights of our visit was the day our daughters – ranging in age from 12 to 14 years old – signed up for whitewater rafting on the Nantahala River. The river is rated as one of the top in the region for water sports.

On the big day, we arrived at the Nantahala Outdoor Center (better known to outdoor enthusiasts as NOC) and began the process of preparing our daughters to have the adventure of the summer! When it was all said and done, they were wet and cold but so excited by their adventure they couldn't stop talking about it for the rest of our vacation.

As I look back on that day, it was, indeed, an amazing experience—but far more for our daughters than for us parents. Why? Because while we *heard* about the adventure, our daughters *experienced* it. We enjoyed hearing their stories. But, clearly, hearing stories pales in comparison with actually getting into the raft and launching into the adventure.

The same is true with the mission of Jesus.

More and more U.S. Christians are focusing on the mission of Jesus in their own community. Perhaps that's why you picked up this book. You've heard about "missional living" and "missional communities," and you love to hear the stories of people on the adventure. But now you are ready to move from hearing the stories to actually getting in the raft and launching into the adventure yourself!

This book, *Joining Jesus on His Mission*, is written for you.

Joining Jesus on His Mission is not so much about missional stories as it is about laying out how to take up a missional lifestyle in a simple, sustainable way. Think of it this way: there are books that tell the stories of whitewater rafting and there are books that show you how to whitewater raft.

This is a book that shows you *how*. It's a field manual that shows you how to take up the mindset and simple practices needed to join Jesus on his redemptive mission in the places you already live, work or go to school.

The first part of this book will focus on the mindset we need to be an everyday missionary. The second part will focus on the practices. In the end you will have what you need to get started on the mission-adventure Jesus has prepared for you (Ephesians 2:10). Not much of a reader? You can go straight to the end of each chapter and catch the summaries called "Here's the Point." These summaries give you the essence of the chapters' content without all the reading. Whichever option you choose, the goal is the same: enabling you to join the mission-adventure into which Jesus is inviting you.

It's your turn to get in the raft.

JOINING
JESUS
ON HIS MISSION

How to Be an
Everyday Missionary

CHAPTER 1
WHAT'S JESUS UP TO?

"The time has come."

— Jesus in Mark 1:15

"So, how's Jesus been messing with you lately?" I was asking this of a pastor I had just met. His response? A knowing smile.

I get that a lot.

My name is Greg Finke, and my wife, Susan, and I have a ministry called Dwelling 1:14. It is a ministry dedicated to helping congregations disciple their people to be neighborhood missionaries. We help leaders connect their people for seeking God's Kingdom and joining his mission in the places they live, work and go to school. It's a lot of fun. The name "Dwelling 1:14" comes from John 1:14, "The Word became flesh and made his dwelling among us." The name reminds us that in order to join Jesus on his redemptive mission, we need to actually be with (dwell with) people who don't yet know him.

As my wife and I travel around the country with Dwelling 1:14, we have the opportunity to meet pastors and people from all types of congregations and communities. And during our initial conversations we often pose the "how's-Jesus-messing-with-you" question. It is a question designed to make them stop and think.

It might help you to know that the phrase "messing with you" is a phrase we use here in the South where I live. It's not a phrase that assumes Jesus has been bullying or picking on someone. It's more along the line of, "How's Jesus been trying to get your attention lately? What's he been showing you? What's he been stirring in you? How has he made you uncomfortable with your status quo?"

And do you know what I'm finding out? Jesus is messing with a lot of us.

People struggle to put it into words, but we're sensing that Jesus is up to something, showing us something new, inviting us to perceive what he is doing *next*. It seems to be right there in front of us and yet still just outside our ability to see clearly or articulate fully. We are like the blind man in Mark 8:22 who is beginning to see but cannot quite make out what he is seeing. It is frustrating and exhilarating all at the same time! We know we are beginning to perceive new things (exhilarating!) but we do not yet have the perception we need to clarify what we are seeing (frustrating!).

Can you relate? You are not alone.

There is a growing sense among the leaders I am talking with that Jesus is up to something, that he's messing with our presumptions, calling us to something more than what we have settled for. He is giving many of us a holy discontent with the status quo so that we will look up from what we are doing, pay attention to him and start to wrestle with what he is currently showing us and asking of us. I hear it as I talk with twenty-somethings in places like Houston, New York City and Portland. I hear it as I talk with retirees in the Midwest and the Deep South. I hear it as I talk with the white pastor in Minneapolis; the Native American pastor in Alaska and the black pastor in New

Orleans. I hear it as I talk with congregational leaders from small towns and big cities, from new churches and 150 year old churches.

Something is coming to a close and something new is coming upon us. And Jesus wants us paying attention.

It's unsettling and uncomfortable. And yet, I think because we sense it is from Jesus, people are also stirred, excited, feeling like an adventure is about to begin. And an adventure *is* about to begin – the adventure of joining Jesus on his redemptive mission to our own community. However, if we're going to be able to follow Jesus into his next adventure, he needs us paying attention to him. Jesus messes with us so that we stop and look around. He wants us to take note of what he is already doing around us. He wants us to look up from our routines and notice that the world is changing and he is already on the move in response.

And why does Jesus need our attention for that? *Because he intends for us to join him.*

In a remarkably short amount of time, the U.S. has become one of the largest mission fields on the planet. The odds are very good that right now, wherever you live in the U.S., the people in your neighborhood and workplace are largely unconnected to a local congregation and may not be connected to Jesus at all. We are no longer a church who is servicing a community filled with a variety of Christians. We are now a church who finds itself needing to be on mission in a mission field.

And we weren't trained for that.

The mindset and practices of our congregations are perfectly calibrated for a U.S. culture that is essentially already gone. The church I grew up in in the 1960s and 1970s was well suited for the largely churched culture that existed in the U.S. at that time. However, in the ensuing decades the U.S. has dramatically shifted from a "churched culture" (where most people go to church or at least know they should go to church) to a "mission field" (where the majority of people do not go to church or feel an obligation to do so). The trouble, of course, is that most churches and church-goers continue to think and operate as if the U.S. culture is still essentially churched and looking for a church home.

And they aren't.

Uh, oh.

This is why so many churches across the country are struggling. The good news is that Jesus isn't struggling and he knows exactly what to do next. In fact, he is already showing us and leading us into his response. And that is the purpose of this book, to help you see what he is already showing you and follow where he is already leading.

In the midst of our unsettled and uncertain world, Jesus is not wringing his hands in worry. He is not confused or discouraged. He is God. And while some of our churchy presumptions and programs may be in trouble, his Church is not. Jesus is very clever. He is using these shifting times to wake us up and get us ready to rejoin him on his redemptive mission to our neighborhoods, workplaces and schools. Not everyone will pay attention and even fewer will respond. But Jesus is moving out on his mission to redeem and restore all people to his Father's kingdom. And he invites us to join him.

"Come, follow me."

Joining Jesus on his redemptive mission is what I mean by the term "missional living." "Missional living" is simply living each day as if it were a mission trip. The difference, of course, is that instead of being on a mission trip to a foreign land, we are on a mission trip to our own community. We are Neighborhood Missionaries. The word "missional" is simply a descriptive word indicating that each part of our daily lives can now be seen as part of Jesus' redemptive mission in our community. Going out to get the mail, going to the store for a gallon of milk or going to the school to pick up our kids now has mission potential.

But don't worry. Joining Jesus on his mission is easier than we think—not more complicated. Joining Jesus doesn't add another layer of busyness on top of an already insane schedule. Instead, joining Jesus results in less stress, more life, more laughter and more fruit than what many of us are currently seeing. Living missionally simply requires a new "missional" mindset – in other words, we begin to think of ourselves as Neighborhood Missionaries – and to put some new "missional" practices into play along the way, which I will describe and unpack in this book.

And congregational leaders, be of good cheer! Joining Jesus on his mission does not require your church to change its worship style (again), or its mission statement or its current constitution. You don't have to switch from an organ to a band or from a band to an organ. Joining Jesus' mission doesn't require installing a whole new layer of programming. It doesn't even require a congregational vote. We don't need to add more staff, build another building or launch a capital campaign.

Joining Jesus' mission is not so much about changing the whole church as it is about changing our own mindset and practices and inviting a few friends to come with us. Think of a "pinch of yeast" as it gradually spreads through "the loaf" of our congregation. We don't try to convince the whole congregation to be "missional," all at once, on the count of three. We start with the few who are ready and willing to come along with us and put the mindset and practices of a Neighborhood Missionary into play as part of our everyday lives. Joining Jesus' mission is not about changing what we do when we go to church on Sunday mornings. It is about changing what we do when we go out as Church into our neighborhoods, workplaces and schools on Monday mornings. And this book will show you how to do that in a simple, sustainable way.

Like my good friend Gary Faith often says, "If we always do what we've always done, we'll always get what we've always gotten." If there was a day when that was acceptable for the U.S. church, it is now gone. Instead, it is time for Jesus' Church to take up the mindset of a missionary with a few missional practices so that, by God's grace, we will get new mission-results.

Old mindset, old practices, old results. New mindset, new practices, new results.

Makes sense.

Are you ready to take up the missional mindset and practices that will put you into position to join Jesus on his redemptive mission every day? By God's grace, as we work our way through this book, we will go from uncertainty to understanding and from anxiety to excitement about living as a Neighborhood Missionary. We will discern a simple plan and take the first steps of joining Jesus on his redemptive mission in the places we already live, work and go to school.

It's why he's been messing with us. So now that he has our attention… "Come, follow me."

Let the adventure begin.

HERE'S THE POINT

How is Jesus messing with you? What is he up to? What is he inviting you to notice, believe or wrestle with? What is he inviting you to *do*? Let's go find out!

CHAPTER 2
JOINING JESUS

"The Word became flesh and blood and moved into the neighborhood."

—John 1:14 (The Message)

Jesus is on a mission. He is on a grand adventure to redeem and restore human lives to the kingdom of his Father. This is nothing new. Ever since he broke out of the tomb on Easter Sunday, Jesus has been on the loose, pursuing his redemptive mission, messing with people, ripening people, preparing people to be drawn back to the Father he loves. It's what he does.

And he's on the move in *your* neighborhood, too.

The concept of "neighborhood" is very important for the missional lifestyle. So let's take a moment to define it. "Neighborhood" is all about the relationships, or the potential relationships, we could have with just a little intentionality. For our purposes a "neighborhood" is defined as any network of people to which we have regular access. Who is regularly within our reach? We may not know the people yet or know them well, but for a variety of reasons these people are regularly within our vicinity. What are some examples of these relational networks we call "neighborhoods?"

Obviously the "neighborhoods" where we live qualify, as do the "neighborhoods" of our workplaces and schools. We are regularly within reach of the same people. But there are many other "neighborhoods" in which we regularly find ourselves. For instance, some of us have access to recreation leagues, yoga classes or craft beer clubs. Some of us are band parents or soccer moms, or we routinely wait with other dads as our daughters finish up dance classes. Some of us volunteer with community revitalization groups or social service agencies. Some of us are Chamber members or Rotary Club members. Some of us are at country clubs, community centers or the Y. All of these are examples of "neighborhoods" in which we may find ourselves. Take a moment to list the "neighborhoods" to which you have access.

Now, here's some important news: Jesus is on the loose in all of them.

How do I know? Because Jesus is on a mission to redeem and restore *all* people. Jesus reminds Nicodemus of this when he spoke the well-known words, "For God so loved the world that he gave his one and only Son ..." (John 3:16). God sent his Son for the *world*. His goal is not to save some and leave others out. Paul underscores this in 1 Timothy 2:4 when he says that God our Savior wants *all* people to be saved. Will everyone respond? Will everyone believe God? No. But that does not change the goal and desire of God in sending his Son. As if to emphasize that very point, God speaks of why he is sending his Son in Isaiah 49:6, "It is too small a thing for you to be my servant to restore the tribes of Jacob and bring back those of Israel I have kept. I will also make you a light for the Gentiles, that you may bring my salvation to the ends of the earth."

So wherever you go, whether to the ends of the earth or just to work, if there are people there, you can be sure Jesus is up to something redemptive. His purpose is to redeem. His goal is full restoration. This is what Jesus does. He doesn't get distracted. He doesn't veer off course. His timing is always precise because his redemptive mission is always what he's up to. Different people. Different timing. Different stories and pathways. Sure. But this is what he is up to all the time.

Think of it this way: every person you see around you has a length of life. You can imagine it like a timeline. They are born. They live their days. They die. And then there is eternity. Jesus intersects every person's timeline at various points during their life in order to begin a process of redemption and restoration to the Kingdom of his Father. This is what Jesus is up to. This is his mission. Now imagine a point on a person's timeline when they believe and receive the Father's forgiveness and restored life. Some people are nearly at that point. Others are far from that point. And, of course, others are well past that point already living life with the Father. However, for those not yet at that point, every day Jesus is working out his plan to prepare them (ripen them) for the day on their timeline when they will receive the good news of redemption and restoration.

There is, of course, much mystery in how Jesus works out his plan in each person's life. But this is what Jesus is up to every day with every person. This is what Jesus is up to in every one of our "neighborhoods." Some people are resisting, some are ignoring, some are oblivious, and some are almost ready. But Jesus is in the redemptive process of uniquely preparing each of them to receive what the Father would freely give them: forgiveness of sins and a new life with him forever.

That is Jesus' mission.

And he invites us to join him.

This is an important change in mindset for most U.S. church members: Jesus is inviting me to join him on his mission. He does not give me a mission to do *for* him. Jesus is on a mission and he invites me to come *with* him. The first time I realized Jesus was inviting me to come *with* him and not go *for* him was a great relief. If I go *for* Jesus, I am doing the work and seeing the results of what I can accomplish. When I go *with* Jesus, he is doing the work and I am seeing the results of what Jesus can accomplish. One is hard, the other is fun. One is exhausting, the other is energizing. One causes me to worry ("Did I do everything correctly?"), the other causes me to be at peace ("Let's see what Jesus does next."). One tempts me to force things with people, the other invites me to keep loving people.

So, for years, when I thought of myself as being in mission, I had it in my head that Jesus was sending me off *for* him ... on my own ... to do the best I could ... which I knew would not be very good at all. I was afraid people would reject me or I wouldn't know what to say, or worse, I would say something and botch the whole deal for Jesus. What a burden! Can you relate? But I had it precisely backwards. Jesus wasn't sending me out to do his work *for* him, he was inviting me to come *with* him and join the work he was already doing.

What a relief! You see, only Jesus can do Jesus-work. So let him. Someone once told me, "I can't. Jesus can. Think I'll let him." Our job isn't to try and do Jesus' work *for* him. Our job is to watch for, recognize and then respond to the work Jesus is already doing in the lives of people around us and *join* him. More on that in chapter seven. Only Jesus can do Jesus-work. Only Jesus could die on the cross and rise again to take away our sins. Only Jesus can ripen a person for this good news. Only Jesus can know the timing of a person's seasons and what's stirring around in the deep places of their heart. Only Jesus can continue to wrestle with someone in their head even when there is no one else around. Only Jesus can cause the seed we sow of kind-attention, gentle-truth or longed-for-grace to germinate at just the right moment.

Jesus is on a mission to redeem and restore human lives to the Kingdom of his Father. This is what he does. And you can count on this: he is already on the move; already doing the heavy lifting of preparing human hearts for good news; already working, stirring, whispering and sometimes shouting to people in all of our "neighborhoods." He wants them to turn their heads and hearts toward his Father ready to receive what he would freely give them.

Jesus speaks of this in John 4 when he says to those with him, "Open your eyes and look at the fields! They are ripe for harvest" (John 4:35). When Jesus says people are "ripe for harvest" he simply means they are "ready for good news from God." Now, if I had been one of the disciples hearing Jesus say this, I would have wondered, "How can anyone be ripe? I haven't done anything yet!" However, Jesus is saying that if, wherever we are, we will open our eyes and look at the people around us, we can know that the Spirit of God has already been at work in their lives long before we arrived on the scene. So, Jesus says, count on it and look for it. God's already been at work in their lives. They may not understand it. They probably don't know it is him. But God has brought many of them to a point where they are "ripe" to encounter his good news. Jesus simply wants us to open our eyes and look for these people.

And what is the good news of God? Certainly the core of God's good news is that he sent his Son Jesus to die on the cross and rise again for the forgiveness of our sins. But what does this *mean*? It means that there is hope. There is forgiveness. There is a better way. God is for us not against us. He has not rejected us or forgotten us. It means we are loved and that we can trust him ... with *everything*.

So, who is ready for good news in your "neighborhoods?"

For many years, my family and I lived in Bullock Creek, Michigan (just outside the town of Midland). Our home was on a small hobby farm. It once had been a working farm, established in 1910. Over the years, through different owners, the original acreage had been sold off. By the time we bought it in 1992, it was down to five acres. But it was just right for us. Folks called it the Finke Farm. One of the things we loved about living on the Finke Farm was the big old trees. And in our front yard was an old apple tree that had been producing apples in that spot for many decades. Having grown up in Houston, Texas, I didn't know much about apple trees.

But here's what I found out.

Apples would form on the tree in early summer. It wouldn't be long before they were fully formed and turning red. However, if I tried to pick an apple too early in the season, it simply would refuse to let go of the branch. In fact, more often than not, before the apple would allow itself to be picked, the twig it was on would snap. I would end up with an apple in my hand and six inches of twig still attached to it. What was the problem? The apples simply were not ready. Now, contrast that with my experience in fall. I would be mowing the grass around my apple tree, and all it would take is a light breeze to cause the apples to start raining down on my head! What was the difference? The apples were now ready.

Here's the mission lesson: if people are not ready, it is almost impossible to pick them. But once they are ready, they'll come looking for you. With the apple tree, I had no way to hurry the ripening process along. All I could do was check on their progress from time to time and be ready when they were finally ripe. The same is true for people. Our job is not to try and hurry people along in the ripening process. Jesus is in charge of ripening people. Our job is to watch for people who are ripe.

Like Eddie did with his friend, Mike.

I met Eddie and Mike during one of our Dwelling 1:14 missional trainings in central Louisiana. When they heard me talking about ripe apples and ripe people they wanted to tell me their story. Eddie and Mike had met years ago when they were police officers. Mike was tall and a natural leader. Eddie was shorter and the funny guy. They both played on the department basketball team and enjoyed hanging out with each other. Eddie knew Jesus' grace. Mike didn't. Mike grew up hearing of God's condemnation and was convinced he was too far gone for heaven to be an option. Mike was thoughtful and a man of honest integrity. When he did the math, he knew he was left out of heaven. So when Eddie would offer Jesus from time to time, Mike would say, "No thanks. There's not much there for me." Eddie wouldn't push it. He was Mike's friend even if Mike did not yet want his Jesus. Then one day, it was time. All of a sudden, for no apparent reason, it was the Holy Spirit's day to get a hold of Mike. Everything suddenly clicked. The light went on spiritually. And when that happened, who did Mike immediately think to go to?

His friend Eddie.

Mike knew that Eddie knew Jesus. And because Eddie hadn't been pushing Mike but had been a friend to Mike, it was the most natural thing in the world for Mike to go to his friend ... when he was ready. Today, Eddie and Mike are still good friends, but now they are on a new adventure together, the adventure of Jesus' redemptive mission. Mike is in the process of becoming a pastor. He's a natural leader. And Eddie? He's still the funny one and still looking for people who are ready.

So open your eyes and look around. Notice the people who are already there. We can be sure Jesus is up to something redemptively in their lives. Some are resisting, some are ignoring, and some are oblivious. But don't miss this: some are ready. And when they are ready, they don't need us telling them *everything* we know about Jesus *all at once*. If they are ready for a little hope or a little grace, they don't need us turning on our Jesus-hose and spraying them down with everything we know about Jesus. They don't need us spraying them down with our Jesus-hose. They need us to offer them a cool-cup-of-water of Jesus.

Do you remember the timeline illustration from earlier in the chapter? Imagine a person is 100 steps away from the moment on their timeline when they step into believing and receiving Jesus. If they are 100 steps away from that moment, they are not ready for the "Jesus-step" just yet (the step when they believe and receive Jesus). However, while they may not be ready for the "Jesus-step," they probably are ready for the "next-step" on the journey *toward* Jesus. And we need to remember, the "next-step" on their journey is as important as the final step on their journey to Jesus. The last step into Jesus' arms can't happen without all those "next-steps" happening first.

What are the early steps people are ready for? Maybe they are ready for a friend who takes time to listen. Maybe they are ready for a friend who is not always in a hurry. Maybe they are ready for a friend who is authentic or has integrity or can be trusted. Each of these may be important steps along their journey. And with each step they become ready for the next step. Are they ready for hope? Are they ready to know they are not alone? Are they ready to know God has not forgotten them? Are they ready to hear their guilt can be forgiven? Are they ready to know there is a better way than what they have settled for? Are they ready for grace?

If we listen, they will tell us. They may not use the literal words, "Will you tell me about hope?" But as they share their questions and worry and struggles, in essence they are asking us that very question. And when they ask us such a question, they are ready for us to be a friend - not a friend who is nervous and trying to remember the right answers, but a friend who is ready for a conversation … a conversation which may occur over weeks or even months. We don't have to have the pressure of wrapping everything up in one conversation. We'll see them again. They live in our "neighborhood."

If they happen to ask a question to which we have no answer, it is a sign of integrity for us to say, "That's a good question. Let me try to find a good answer."

This is our new missional mindset: We know Jesus is already out there in our "neighborhoods" doing the heavy lifting of ripening people for their next step towards his Father's redemption. So every morning, as we head out for a new day of mission-adventure with Jesus, we can ask ourselves these simple questions:

What's Jesus already up to?

Who are these people around me?

And what are they almost ready for?

Jesus did not give you a mission to do *for* him. He invites you to come on his mission *with* him. This is our new missional mindset. We can do this.

Let's find out how.

HERE'S THE POINT

Jesus is on a mission and he invites you to join him. He does not give you a mission to do *for* him. He is on a mission and invites you to come *with* him.

Now let's turn our attention to this mission field we call the United States of America.

CHAPTER 3
THE RIVER MOVED

"We lost in 72 hours what we have taken more than 50 years to build, bit by bit."

—Honduran President Carlos Flores
in the aftermath of Hurricane Mitch

It took me a moment to realize what I was looking at. I was online and looking at a photograph of a river and a bridge taken from an airplane. But something was obviously wrong. The bridge was missing the river! The photograph showed a perfectly good bridge situated *beside* the river. Not *over* the river like normal bridges but *beside* the river. It looked like someone had gone to all the trouble of building a bridge, but then forgot the main job of a bridge is to span a river! What a dumb mistake! Who would build a bridge in the wrong place?

However, there was more to the story of this river and bridge than met the eye.

You see, what I was looking at was the Choluteca Bridge in Honduras. It was a state-of-the-art bridge built by a Japanese firm for the Honduran government. When built, it did, indeed, perfectly span the Choluteca River. However, in October 1998, a tropical storm formed and began to gain strength in the western Caribbean Sea. It would soon reach hurricane strength and be called Mitch. Hurricane Mitch grew at one point to be a category five hurricane, the most powerful level of storm. However, by the time it approached the Honduran coast it had weakened to a category one hurricane. Mitch then essentially stalled and, over the next few days, sat there churning over Honduras, dumping historic amounts of rain on the region. There were reports of up to 75 inches of rain in some areas. That's over six feet of water!

Honduras is a mountainous region, and when all that water came crashing down out of the mountains and into the Choluteca River Valley, it did so with such ferocity that it literally changed the course of the river. In a matter of days, a perfectly good, well-built, well-placed bridge became obsolete ... and frankly, years later, looks pretty silly sitting there missing the river. (If you'd like, you can take a look at the photograph yourself by doing an online image search using the words "Choluteca Bridge after hurricane.")

However, here's the point: The real problem isn't that someone built the wrong bridge in the wrong place. The problem is that the river moved.

When I think about how quickly the U.S. has become a major mission field, it is stunning. In fact, it is so stunning that many people have a hard time getting their minds around it. They struggle to understand the scope of this reality and the implications for their local congregations. Because of that struggle, I have found it helpful to use the picture of the Choluteca Bridge as a metaphor for what has happened to the U.S. church. Here's why.

For years we were able to build and operate churches as important centers of our culture. When people established a new community, one of the first buildings constructed was a church. When a family came to a new community, one of the first things they sought out was a church home. During most of the twentieth century, the U.S. saw itself as a Christian nation. Churches were important. Churches were respected. Churches helped set the agenda and atmosphere for their local communities. There really wasn't a need for a church to strategize how to "reach" its community because all they had to do was schedule a service on Sunday, open the doors and people would come!

For a very long time the U.S. church was well-built, well-positioned and doing an excellent job of meeting the spiritual needs of a largely churched culture. We could say the church was "spanning the river" of the U.S. culture at that time. However, over the last 40 or so years, a cultural and religious hurricane has been churning over the U.S. leaving the landscape unrecognizable to Christians who came of age before the 1970s.

The river moved.

The "river" of the U.S. culture has shifted away from the "bridge" of the U.S. church as dramatically as the Choluteca River shifted away from the bridge during hurricane Mitch. For the first time in U.S. history, congregations can no longer rely on a strategy of attracting people to religious services as being the best means of introducing people to the Gospel. People in the community are increasingly saying, "No, thank you," to our invitations to come to church. Previous assumptions and strategies that used to work well are suddenly not working so well anymore.

Consider the following:

1. Surveys reveal that over the last few decades literally millions of people who previously were members of churches have walked away.

2. Even in so-called "churched" communities, the percentage of "church-goers" actually attending worship on any given Sunday hovers between 18-22%.

3. The number of Americans who say they have no religious affiliation has hit an all-time high.

4. Confidence in organized religion has hit an all-time low.

5. Less than 10% of adults under 30 regularly participate in the life of a local congregation. In overwhelming numbers, young adults perceive the organized church to be unnecessary to their spiritual journey.

I get a heart-breaking reminder of this every time I am with a group of older Christians and I ask, "How many of you have children or grandchildren who no longer worship regularly?" In most cases many hands go up. They all have a story of heartache to tell.

So how could this happen? How is it that a perfectly good, well-placed church like we had just a couple decades ago could so quickly become obsolete to the culture in general and our own children and grandchildren specifically?

The river moved.

For a very long time the U.S. church was well-built, well-positioned and doing an excellent job of "spanning the river" of U.S. culture. The churches we built, the strategies we followed and the presumptions we had were right for the culture that existed at the time. However, the river moved.

Looking at the problem of the Choluteca Bridge, it is obvious that the solution is not to try and make the river move back to where it was. The solution is to build the next span of bridge over where the river is now. In the same way, our solution as the church is not to try and make the U.S. culture move back to where it was, but to focus our prayer and planning on building the next span of bridge over where the culture is now.

And where is it now?

In a remarkably short amount of time, the U.S. has become one of the largest mission fields in the world. In fact, with each generation of new Americans we are moving further beyond being even a "post-churched" culture (those who were raised in church but no longer participate) to being a "pre-churched" culture (those who were not raised with church at all).

Do you know what that makes us? Missionaries.

Here's what I mean: Because I am a Jesus-follower living in the mission field of the U.S., that makes me a missionary, whether I realize it or not. We used to think of missionaries as being sent to the mission fields of far-off places like Africa and China. But now we can send missionaries to the mission fields of our own subdivisions, neighborhoods and apartment complexes. We used to think of people as being "overseas missionaries." But now we can think of people as being "neighborhood missionaries." We used to think that if someone became a missionary, we would send them to India or South America. Now we can simply send them home after worship because our local neighborhoods have become mission fields.

Ironically, in the same span of decades that the U.S. has become a major mission field, the major mission fields of the world have become much more Christian. Today, there are nearly as many Lutherans in Ethiopia as there are in the U.S. There are now more Baptists in Nagaland (an eastern state in India) than there are in the southern states of the U.S. There were more Christians worshiping in China last Sunday than there were here in the U.S. or in all of Europe! So what does this mean for us? In a matter of decades church people have become missionaries in our own hometowns. The bad news is that we were not raised or discipled to be missionaries! The good news is that Jesus knows this and has made provision for it.

Consider this: the U.S. culture, although remarkably unchurched these days, is also becoming uniquely ripe for the church to be the Church again. What our culture is longing for is actually well within our sweet-spot as Jesus-followers! Our culture may no longer be interested in our "Churchianity" but, without even knowing it, they are uniquely ready for biblical "Christianity." They are looking for what Jesus has already called his followers to be.

For instance:

- People take note when someone is willing to sacrifice themselves for the good of others
- People appreciate the opportunity to sort through their spiritual questions honestly without manipulation
- People are intrigued by someone who exhibits both grace and wisdom
- People are looking for those who exhibit authentic love, joy, peace, patience, kindness and self-control
- They cheer redemptive action
- They wish to discover what is true
- They long for authentic community with people they can trust

- They are wondering if an encounter with a loving God is possible

All this is well within our sweet-spot as Jesus-followers, correct?

The bad news is that people in our culture no longer believe they will find these things in our churches. Maybe they are right, maybe they are wrong. Either way, our culture is looking to the church less and less to meet these longings. So if our churches are operating on the presumption and strategy that the best way to reach our culture with the gospel is by getting people to come to our buildings for religious services and programs, we are probably experiencing more and more disappointment. Things just aren't working like they once did.

The good news is that Jesus has uniquely ripened the culture for the Church to once again go and *be* the Church in our neighborhoods, workplaces and schools. If the culture won't come to our church buildings, the Church can go to them and embody the very things for which they are longing. That's actually how Jesus had always designed his Church to operate, being the people through whom the grace and truth of God is experienced by others in real life.

Every Sunday, Christians gather in worship around Jesus through his Word and sacraments. Then we are sent out to join Jesus as he carries out his redemptive mission in our community the rest of the week. Joining Jesus on this mission is what we mean by "living missionally." Our lives become marked by his mission. We start watching with missional eyes, we start listening with missional ears, we start responding to the people around us with missional responses. That is, we do all those things because we are on Jesus' mission with him. We are living missionally. This is the ancient rhythm of God's people, gathering and going, coming together for worship and going back out for mission, coming to church on Sunday and *being* the Church on Monday.

And it is all the more important now that the river has moved.

The dramatic move in U.S. culture is hard to take. We can grieve it but we can no longer afford to ignore it. It's time for us to sit up and realize we are a missional church in the mission field called the United States of America. That makes you and me missionaries in our own neighborhoods. And although this is new to us it is not new to Jesus.

The river has moved, but Jesus is ready. We can trust him. We cannot make the river go back, but we can join Jesus as he leads us forward to build the next span. All we have to do is become missionaries in the places we already live, work and go to school.

And it's simpler than we think.

HERE'S THE POINT

It's hard to take, but it is what it is. The river has moved. You are a missionary to your own community. It's time to trust Jesus and join him in building the next span of bridge to our current U.S. culture.

CHAPTER 4

ARE YOU STALLING?

"Anyone who has grabbed a bull by the tail knows five or six more things than someone who has not."

—Mark Twain

I like stalling. I don't mean to. It's just that when I am faced with something I am afraid might be hard to do or complicated to figure out, my first instinct is to put it off. However, I have also found that stalling can have an unintended consequence. It can keep you from finding out how simple and fun something is.

I have a friend who put off learning to play golf for years because she thought it would be too hard and complicated. She finally took lessons after her husband retired and began insisting that she golf with him so they could do something active together. Do you know what she found out? She's good at golf. To her husband's chagrin, after a few months of lessons and practice she was better at the game than he was! Stalling all those years kept her from finding out how simple and fun golf could be.

Have you been stalling missionally? In other words, have you been putting off joining Jesus on his mission because you are afraid it is too hard or complicated? I have good news for you! You can stop stalling. Joining Jesus on his mission – that is, living missionally – is simple.

Chances are good that you already know most of what you need to know and just didn't realize it. Joining Jesus on his mission is primarily about taking on the simple mindset we spoke about in chapter two and putting a few simple practices into play as part of our daily life. (We will explore those practices beginning in chapter eleven.) Therefore, joining Jesus on his mission will not require us to absorb a lot of additional teaching. It is simpler than we think, not more complicated. After all, the mission of Jesus originally exploded with "unschooled, ordinary men" (Acts 4:13).

In the end, joining Jesus' mission doesn't require us to know more than we already do but to do more with what we already know.

For instance, a key aspect of living missionally is loving our neighbors as ourselves. We don't really need to know more about the teaching "love your neighbor as yourself" in order to love our neighbors. Our challenge is not a lack of knowledge. It is a lack of action. To put it bluntly, we will see more significant mission happening with our neighbors if we actually love our neighbors than if we merely study more about it.

Another way U.S. Christians stall missionally is when we readily substitute reading another book for actually doing something with what we have already read. Reading so we know what to do is good. Reading so we can put off doing what we know we are to do is not good. Sometimes fear can make us feel like we need to know more before we can actually do something. So we seek out that next book, that next article, that next blog just to make sure we haven't missed something. But ... you know what we are really doing? We're stalling.

My wife, Susan, and I regularly lead day-long trainings on missional living through our ministry called Dwelling 1:14. During the trainings we place a premium on putting the training into practice as soon as the people return home. At the end of one such training, a pastor raised his hand and asked, "Do you have a book you could recommend on this?" Do you see what he was unintentionally doing? He was saying, "Let me read one more book so I can put off actually doing this." In response to his question, I said, "Sure. There are dozens of books. Hundreds, probably. But after you have read the last book, you will still need to actually do something." He laughed. We laughed. Everyone in the room laughed, because we all knew what was really happening. He was stalling.

The bottom line is this: We can read every book there is on mission and missional living. We can study every missional practice, program and paradigm that is published. We can keep investigating the various expressions of missional community as they emerge. But at the end of all our reading, we will still have to actually do something in order to make a missional difference in the life of a real human being. But that's the point: nothing will happen in real lives until we actually do something with what we know.

So remember this truism: it's not what you know that will change the world, but what you do with what you know that will change the world.

Oh.

Which leads to a final insight: Doing mission accelerates our understanding of mission. I have found that we learn much more about missional living – and learn it much more quickly – when we press beyond simply reading about missional practices and start putting them into play in real life. You see, "doing" accelerates "understanding." Yes, reading is important for new insights; however, I have found that the sooner we put insights into action the sooner and more deeply we will understand the mindset and practices we are putting into play. In other words, by giving the mindset and practices a try, as best we can, even though imperfectly, we learn so much more than if we settle for reading about it.

That's what Jesus did with his disciples in Luke 9:1. In this passage we read about Jesus sending his disciples out to preach the kingdom of God. Did Jesus send them out because they already understood so much about the kingdom? Of course not. It was only chapter nine. They still had a lot to learn! Jesus didn't send them out because they already understood so much. He sent them out because they had so much more to understand. Jesus knew that by going and putting his teaching into play they will come to a much deeper understanding of what he has already been teaching them. Doing accelerates understanding.

One of my favorite Mark Twain quotes is, "Anyone who has grabbed a bull by the tail knows five or six more things than someone who has not." A person can read a book about grabbing a bull by the tail but he will not know nearly as much as the person who has actually grabbed one. Likewise, the novelist Dean Koontz has a character named Odd Thomas who puts it this way, "By doing, I learn what to do. By going, I learn where to go." Missional living is new to most of us. Maybe we have been reading about it, thinking about it, even teaching the concepts behind it. But few have been intentionally living it. That means we are inexperienced and that makes us nervous. We know we don't know what we are doing. We are afraid we may do something wrong. So remember this: "By doing, I learn what to do. By going, I learn where to go."

After reading this book, you will know all you need to know to get started. And that's the key to learning the new mindset and practices: starting. If you just start, as best you can, in spite of your fear of messing up, Jesus will be able to show you so much more than if you settle for reading about it, thinking about it, or, in other words, stalling. I remind myself often, "Greg, Jesus knows you're a numbskull." That keeps me from straying into thinking I have to do everything perfectly or I will mess stuff up for Jesus. Jesus knows I am a numbskull. He wasn't counting on me being perfect. He was counting on me being me. And, in his grace, using me in his redemptive mission.

Jesus is pretty cool that way.

I don't know who said it, but I agree with it, "It's better to do something imperfectly than to do nothing flawlessly." Remember, you're joining Jesus on *his* mission. He's already doing the heavy lifting. You're not going out *for* him; you're going out *with* him. So, read the rest of this book. Then resist the urge to do more reading and, instead, put into play the insights you have already gained.

That's how you will move from "thinking about mission" to "joining Jesus' mission."

HERE'S THE POINT

Stop stalling. You will learn more about being a missionary by doing something missional than you will by reading something missional. It's not what you know, but what you do with what you know that makes a difference in people's lives.

CHAPTER 5
COULD IT BE THIS SIMPLE?

"Disturb us, Lord, when we are too pleased with ourselves,
When our dreams have come true because we dreamed too little,
When we arrived safely because we sailed too close to the shore.

"Disturb us, Lord, when with the abundance of things we possess
We have lost our thirst for the waters of life;
Having fallen in love with life, we have ceased to dream of eternity.

"Disturb us, Lord, to dare more boldly,
To venture on wilder seas where storms will show your mastery;
Where losing sight of land, we shall find the stars."

—The prayer of Sir Francis Drake, adventurer (1577)

So, are you nervous yet? If you're like most people, when you start to think about personally being a missionary in the places you already live, work or go to school it can give you the willies. We sense the complexity of the work. We have a pretty good idea that if we took on the challenge of redeeming and restoring our community by ourselves, it could end badly for everyone involved. And yet the mission of redeeming and restoring this beautiful, broken world is still calling us, messing with us, inspiring us to do ... *something*. We read the prayer of Sir Francis Drake above, the sixteenth century English sea captain and adventurer, and we realize we want that same kind of missional "disturbance."

"Disturb us, Lord, when we are too pleased with ourselves, when our dreams have come true because we dreamed too little, when we arrived safely because we sailed too close to the shore."

On the one hand, we no longer can abide the status quo of ignoring the redemptive needs around us. We, too, are stirred to pray, *"Disturb us, Lord, to dare more boldly, to venture on wilder seas."* And yet, on the other hand, to move out beyond the status quo of our daily lives in order to join the mission of Jesus is, well, *disturbing*. We know how complex our world is. It is both beautiful beyond imagination and diabolically broken in ways that crush and swallow mere human beings. Our world is filled with people living in the mix and crush of this complexity – each person's individual story adding to the complexity of the beauty and brokenness around us every day.

I am reminded of this each time I go to outdoor art festivals. My wife and I enjoy being a part of the wonderfully varied and complex mix of humanity that such events invite. It is beautiful and fun to stroll through the booths taking in the various expressions of art – so many insights to what the artists see and feel, so many creative ways to express the human heart and condition. However, in the midst of the beauty it is also easy to see pain and brokenness, some of it of the darkest kind. At art festivals, it's all there to see – the beauty and brokenness of the human family, what brokenness has done but also what redemption could do.

I am reminded of this each time I go to a middle school. I look around at the young people who are streaming in and out of the doors. They are no longer little children but they are not yet young adults. So much beauty and value in each person. So much potential embodied in each young life. Such an impressive display of the creative variety of

God. However, in the midst of the beauty and variety, it is also easy to see how the brokenness of this world is starting to grind into their young souls. Too many of them are learning to live with hopelessness and are giving up on the notion of their worth. At a middle school it's all there to see – the beauty and brokenness of the human family. It is not hard to see what brokenness has done but it is not hard to imagine what redemption could restore.

As I stand back at an art festival or a school, and see both the beauty and pain exhibited, I ask myself, "What would be 'good news' to these people? What aspect of the gospel would bring some healing to their wounds and restoration to their lives?" Each person's life is a complex and unique story of beauty and brokenness. Working out the redemption and restoration for any *one* of these people would be complex beyond measure.

But for *all* people?

To sort out and make right all that has been ruined and lost for all people throughout time is so overwhelmingly complex it can only be worked out by the Son of God himself. And so he does. Jesus himself takes on the overwhelmingly complex work of setting all things right again for *each* person and for *all* people. Those at art fairs, middle schools and in our neighborhoods.

That's what Jesus meant when he said his amazing words in John 3:16, "For God so loved the world that he gave his one and only Son, that whoever believes in him shall not perish but have eternal life." In other words, this world of humanity is perishing, and yet it is the world our God so loved. So, through the love of the Father and the work of the Son, the once-beautiful world of humanity will not be left to its own ruin and destruction. Through the Son, the world the Father so loved will be saved, renewed and restored again. In fact, that is the very exclamation of God at the conclusion of all things. "Behold, I am making everything new!" (Revelation 21:5).

And Jesus wants us to join him in this restorative work. This invitation is both wonderfully exciting to us and deeply disturbing. Therefore, as we noted in chapter two, it is of the highest importance that we listen carefully to how Jesus divides up the work that needs to be done:

- Jesus does the incredibly complex work that requires the Son of God;

- we do the incredibly simple work that requires a little child.

Jesus knows he must keep our role and participation simple. And so he does.

He keeps it as simple as this:

In order to join Jesus on his redemptive mission all we really have to do is:

- enjoy people;

- and seek, recognize and respond to what Jesus is already doing in the lives of the people we are enjoying.

Could it really be this simple? The answer is, "Yes."

Only Jesus, the Son of God, can do the immense and complex work of renewing and restoring all things. However, with a sort of mischievous grace, he has decided to include us in that renewing and restoring in simple but important ways. In the next chapter we will look at why the simple work of "enjoying people" is so important to the redemptive mission of Jesus. Then in chapter seven we will look at what it means to "seek, recognize and respond to what Jesus is already doing in the lives of people we are enjoying."

HERE'S THE POINT

Jesus has made our participation in his redemptive mission simple. Let's keep it that way. We make it hard when we try to do the work of Jesus rather than what he gave us to do.

CHAPTER 6
AN INEFFICIENTLY EFFECTIVE STRATEGY

"He has gone to be the guest of a sinner."

—What all the people muttered as Jesus went to Zacchaeus' house

Did you know that Jesus had a secret weapon for fulfilling his redemptive mission? And it is simple enough for you and me to imitate. Do you know what it was?

He enjoyed hanging out with people.

Have you ever noticed that in the Gospels? If you start looking for it, you might be surprised at how often you find Jesus hanging out with people and enjoying a meal at their home (Luke 7:36), or telling stories to folks gathered around (Mark 4), or attending parties and celebrations with friends and neighbors (John 2 and 12).

The Gospels indicate that Jesus hung out with people *a lot*.

Consider this: in Matthew 11:19, Jesus says, "The Son of Man came eating and drinking, and they say, 'Here is a glutton and a drunkard, a friend of tax collectors and "sinners."'" How did Jesus get that reputation? I'm pretty sure it wasn't because Jesus actually over-ate or over-drank. However, I do know he often hung out with people who did. Some examples: Matthew 9:10, "While having dinner at Matthew's house, many tax collectors and 'sinners' came and ate with him and his disciples." Luke 15:1-2, "Now the tax collectors and 'sinners' were all gathering around to hear Jesus. But the Pharisees and the teachers of the law muttered, 'This man welcomes sinners and eats with them.'" Luke 19:5-7, "Jesus said, 'Zacchaeus, come down immediately. I must stay at your house today.' All the people saw this and began to mutter, 'He has gone to be the guest of a "sinner."'"

Jesus enjoyed being with people and knew how to hang out with them. He watched, listened, shared stories and shared life. *He wasn't in a hurry*. And when the moment eventually came to share with them some good news about God, it was well received precisely because he had earned their trust as he hung out with them.

Perhaps most noteworthy is that Jesus chose to hang out with people and enjoy them even though he had a huge mission to accomplish and a limited amount of time with which to accomplish it. So here's the question: Did Jesus choose to hang out with people *in spite* of having a huge mission with limited time or *because* he had a huge mission with limited time? In my view, he hung out with people *because* of it. As we watch Jesus in the Gospels, he seems to choose to hang out with people and enjoy them as the most effective way of accomplishing his huge mission with limited time. Such a strategy seems unlikely to those of us who are busy, goal-oriented people. We don't have time to spare! Hanging out with people seems inefficient to us in the extreme! However, please take note: Jesus chose this strategy for a reason. Could it be that a strategy which on the surface seems inefficient ultimately is most effective? Or to put the question another way: If you have what you consider a more efficient mission strategy than hanging out with people, how's that working for you? Maybe Jesus was on to something after all.

Allow me to explain.

Jesus indirectly addresses this very question at the end of his statement in Matthew 11:19. First Jesus says, "The Son of Man came eating and drinking, and they say, 'Here is a glutton and a drunkard, a friend of tax collectors and "sinners."'" Then he goes on to say, "But wisdom is proved right by her deeds." The New Living Translation translates this verse, "But wisdom is shown to be right by what results from it." In other words, what may not seem like a wise strategy to begin with, will be shown to be spot-on and wise in the end. The result of our strategy proves the wisdom of our strategy. Consider the following list of people: The tax collectors and sinners, Nicodemus, Mary Magdalene, Zacchaeus, the woman at the well and the disciples themselves. This list reads like a Hall of Fame for mission effectiveness. And, yet, each of these people was the result of Jesus' inefficient use of time, namely, hanging out and enjoying them as people.

For busy U.S. Christians, one of the biggest challenges we have in living missionally is investing time in the process of becoming friends with people. We think we need to be efficient with our time. And for many of us, investing in friendship may not seem efficient. We tend to value efficiency over relationship. If we are going to spend time with people missionally we want to be able to accomplish something as efficiently as possible. We calculate it like this, "How much can we accomplish missionally with the least amount of time invested?" That's efficient. Unfortunately, while that logic looks good on paper, dealing efficiently with people for the sake of mission is completely ineffective. (Like I asked earlier, "How's that working for you?") In the U.S., we value efficiency over relationship. In the Gospels, Jesus values relationship over efficiency.

And he seems pretty effective.

As counterintuitive as it sounds, it is the inefficient investment in friendship (being a "friend of sinners") that leads to effective missional results in people's lives. Consider, what would Jesus' mission-work have looked like had he done it our way? On the other hand, what would our mission-work look like if we did it his way? Is it time to put aside our ineffective goal of efficiency and start being with people again?

Hanging out and enjoying people was Jesus' secret weapon for winning the world to his Father. It's easy to underestimate its importance, but it's hard to dismiss its results. Perhaps instead of dismissing the importance of Jesus' hanging out and enjoying people, we should imitate him. Bottom line? Turns out accomplishing missional results efficiently (that is, with minimal investment of time) is ineffective because efficiency doesn't value relationship. On the other hand, as inefficient as building friendships and trust may seem, it is by far the most effective (and enjoyable) way to join Jesus on his mission.

Could joining Jesus on his mission really be this simple? Yes. After all, "Wisdom is proved right by her deeds."

As we saw earlier, Jesus' mission of redeeming and restoring broken people is complex work. That's why he keeps our role and participation simple. In order to join Jesus on his redemptive mission all we have to do is:

- enjoy people;
- and seek, recognize and respond to what Jesus is already doing in the lives of the people we are enjoying.

Why do I use the phrase "enjoy people" rather than a more common phrase like "love people?" After all, doesn't Jesus himself say, "Love your neighbor as yourself?" Of course he does. Here's the reason: U.S. Christians have become good at loving our neighbors "technically" without "actually" loving our neighbors. For instance, we feel confident in saying that we "love our neighbor," yet we often do not even know our neighbor's name. We readily say that we "love our neighbor," yet we neglect acting with any specific love toward the person who actually lives next door to us. We see nothing wrong with drawing distinctions such as, "I love my neighbor, but that doesn't mean I have to like my neighbor."

Really? Where did we get that idea?

When Jesus said, "Love your neighbor as yourself," did he mean we could "technically" love our neighbor without having to "actually" love our neighbor? As we have been pointing out, Jesus was known as a friend of sinners. Evidently, the sinners liked hanging out with Jesus. Do you think they liked being with Jesus because he "loved" them without really "liking" them? Would they have appreciated Jesus if he had simply "put up with them" rather than genuinely enjoying them? "Technical" love doesn't feel like love at all. Real love doesn't ignore their neighbor or simply put up with their neighbor. Real love enjoys their neighbor and is a friend to their neighbor.

Where did we get that crazy idea?

Jesus.

Jesus didn't ignore sinners or put up with sinners. Jesus enjoyed sinners and was a friend of sinners. The Gospels show he was actually *there* for them.

But here's a question I am frequently asked: "What if I genuinely do not like my neighbor?" That's a good question. What if we have had issues with our neighbor? What if they've been unkind or coarse or even criminal? How can we enjoy someone who is a "sinner" to us? Jesus shows us the answer: We do what Jesus did in order to be *our* friend. And what did he do? He drew deeply upon his Father's grace. In order for Jesus to be our friend he first had to have grace for us. Likewise, in order for us to be friends with the neighbors we don't yet like, we need to draw upon the Father's grace – perhaps deeply. As followers of Jesus we don't put up with our neighbors. We press into his grace and extend friendship to them.

In fact, Jesus says it's good for us.

In Luke 6:32-35 Jesus says, "If you love those who love you, what credit is that to you? Even the 'sinners' love those who love them. And if you do good to those who are good to you, what credit is that to you? Even 'sinners' do that. And if you lend to those from whom you expect repayment, what credit is that to you? Even 'sinners' lend to 'sinners,' expecting to be repaid in full. But love your enemies, do good to them, and lend to them without expecting to get anything back. Then your reward will be great, and you will be sons of the Most High, because he is kind to the ungrateful and wicked." What Jesus is saying is, when a relationship requires us to draw deeply from his grace to be a friend to those who don't deserve it, we are showing ourselves to be children of our heavenly Father. He is also kind to those who don't deserve it. His invitation is not for us to draw just enough grace so that we can "put up with" such neighbors. His invitation is for us to draw enough grace to begin *enjoying* such neighbors.

Grace enables us to see beyond the irritations and frustrations our neighbor is causing us – even the neighbor who has set himself up as our enemy. Grace enables us to see the neighbor *as a person*, not just as the trouble he is causing us. In grace, Jesus sees redemptive value in our neighbor. That's why Jesus loved our neighbor and gave his life for him. With such grace, we can now begin to go well beyond "putting up with" our neighbor and begin enjoying our neighbor ... which looks a lot more like the "actual" love of which Jesus speaks.

As we begin to employ Jesus' inefficiently effective strategy of hanging out and enjoying people, we need to be aware of a temptation. The temptation is to offer our friendship to people *only* if they will receive our Jesus in return (or at least be nice to us). It goes something like this, "I will love you as long as there is a chance you will respond properly and start loving Jesus the way I do." Unfortunately, this is an easy temptation for us. It is especially easy to fall into if we are still longing for an efficient investment of our missional time. (After all, who has time for people who won't be nice to us or come to faith *quickly*?) Instead, Jesus invites us to offer our friendship and time to people even if they don't yet want him. Why? Because that's what Jesus did.

I call the kind of friendship Jesus offered "agenda-less friendship." Agenda-less friendship is authentic friendship offered simply for the sake of being friends. It is friendship offered before any assurances can be given that the friend will come to faith. A good example of this is Nicodemus, who first meets with Jesus at night in John 3. This meeting happened at the beginning of Jesus' ministry. Jesus and Nicodemus had an intense conversation that night, but one gets the impression Nicodemus left unconvinced. Evidently he was not yet ready to believe who Jesus was. Nevertheless, Jesus offered him friendship and time. Why? Jesus' time and friendship paved the way for the Holy Spirit to do his work in Nicodemus' heart – not quickly but eventually. We know this because we encounter Nicodemus again at the *end* of Jesus' ministry. In a poignant scene recorded in John 19:39, we find

Nicodemus accompanying Joseph of Arimathea to the cross. Together they remove Jesus' dead body from the cross and prepare it for burial. Jesus' friendship and the work of the Holy Spirit have had their effect on Nicodemus. He is ready to believe Jesus.

In John 3 Jesus is showing Nicodemus agenda-less friendship. An inefficient way for Jesus to spend an evening? Perhaps. However, "wisdom is proved right by her deeds." Friendship offered as a gift of grace may seem inefficient at first but in the end it is the only way to create the *opportunity* for a response even though a response may be very slow in coming – like with Nicodemus. Friendship that is offered with an ulterior agenda (even a good agenda) is no friendship at all. It is bait. If a person finally catches on to what is really happening, they feel snookered and used. ("Oh. So that's what's really going on here?")

I was once invited to lunch by a person who originally claimed they wanted to meet me and get to know me. I was honored, since this person was a person of some standing in our community. Unfortunately, as the lunch progressed, it became increasingly obvious they had no real interest in my friendship. They wanted access to my congregation's phone directory. I thought, "Oh. So that's what is really going on here?" I felt snookered and used. The person was offering friendship (sort of) for my directory. That's an example of someone offering "agenda-full friendship."

William Young, author of *The Shack* wrote, "You are free to live and love without any agenda, making your life and your love much more trustworthy." If we love with an agenda, our love is untrustworthy because it is really bait. If we love with an agenda, we will value our agenda more than the person. If we love with an agenda, the temptation will be to become increasingly manipulative in order to *make* them comply. If, after a time, they don't comply with our agenda, we will withdraw our love. "It didn't work," we think to ourselves. But that's not the way Jesus loves. He loves because every person needs love whether they receive it or not. 1 John 4:19 says it plainly, "We love because he first loved us," not because people have earned our love by conforming to our agenda.

Our only "agenda" – if you want to call it that – is Jesus' agenda. Jesus has an agenda for every person that redeems all their losses and restores their lives to his Father's kingdom. *How* that agenda gets worked out and the *timing* of that agenda is Jesus' work alone. An agenda of our making is a shot in the dark. Jesus' agenda is a plan from eternity. An agenda of our making is ultimately manipulative. Jesus' agenda is ultimately redemptive. Our "agenda" is to have no other agenda than to enjoy the person and watch for how Jesus unfolds *his* agenda. As one person once told me, "To have no agenda is so freeing for me! All I have to do is be there to enjoy the person and then respond to what Jesus is doing in their lives."

Correct. (More on "responding" in the next chapter.)

Enjoying people frees us from needing any other "agenda" for people. I remember a person once telling me how their friend turned serious one day and said, "Don't make me your project." That struck me. Their friend was sending a clear message that "being fixed" felt demeaning. It caused me to wrestle again with the difference between trying to "fix" people as a project and being with people as a friend ... like Jesus was when he hung out with people. Being an agenda-less friend to someone doesn't mean we disregard right and wrong or wisdom and foolishness. It doesn't mean we sit idly by as people hurt themselves with self-defeating or self-destructive choices. It doesn't mean we forget that "the truth will set you free."

We are an agenda-less friend when we realize that we really can't control our friend or make their decisions for them (think of Jesus with Nicodemus). What we *can* do is enjoy them and watch for what Jesus is up to in their life. What we *can* do is be convinced of their value as a child of God even when they make choices that demean it. What we *can* do is love our friend enough to tell them the truth and then love our friend enough to stay with them even when they make a crazy-bad decision anyway.

What we *can* do is imitate Jesus.

"The Son of Man came eating and drinking, and they say, 'Here is a glutton and a drunkard, a friend of tax collectors and "sinners."'" Could joining Jesus on his mission really be this simple?

Yes. After all, "Wisdom is proved right by her deeds."

HERE'S THE POINT

It really is this simple. Jesus' secret weapon for accomplishing his redemptive mission was hanging out with sinners and enjoying them in his Father's grace. It was inefficiently effective. We can question this strategy, but Jesus would have us imitate it.

Next, let's see what Jesus tells us about "seeking, recognizing and responding" to what he is already doing in the lives of the people we have started enjoying.

CHAPTER 7
SEEKING WHAT'S ALREADY HAPPENING

"He who keeps on seeking finds ..."
—Jesus in Matthew 7:8 (AMP)

How do we seek, recognize and respond to what Jesus is already doing in the lives of the people we are enjoying?

Most people I talk with think this must be the most difficult, mysterious part of joining Jesus on his mission. After all, isn't Jesus invisible? How do you seek an invisible person? Likewise, wouldn't recognizing the movement of the Spirit of Jesus require an unusually high level of spiritual maturity or at least skill? Turns out seeking and recognizing what Jesus is doing in the lives of people around us is pretty simple. After all, we are not being asked to seek what *isn't* happening right before our eyes but to simply seek what *is* happening right before our eyes.

All we have to do is look.

If we don't look, of course, we won't find. That's why a lot of us, at this point at least, don't know what Jesus is doing in the lives of people around us. It's not that there is nothing to see. It's that so few of us are looking for it. But if we will seek, Jesus says in Matthew 7:8, we will find. A more precise translation of this verse would be, "He who *keeps on seeking* finds ..." In the original Greek, Jesus uses an ongoing verb tense for *seek*, indicating that our action of seeking is to be a persistent habit not an occasional hobby. Jesus promises that those who will continue seeking will find what God is showing them.

As far back as Jeremiah, God promised that this day would come, "'You will seek me and find me when you seek me *with all your heart* [emphasis mine]. I will be found by you,' declares the LORD," (Jeremiah 29:13-14).

So, how do we seek, recognize and respond to what Jesus is already doing in the lives of the people we are enjoying? We start paying attention to what is already being shown us. Pretty simple. However, having said that, it is simple for very complex reasons. What do I mean by that? Consider this: Jumping into the car and driving to the store is simple for me. All I have to do is put the key in the ignition; shift the car into gear and drive off to the store. Driving to the store is simple for me. The *reason* it is simple for me is very complex for many other people. Thousands of highly skilled people had to figure out how to make all kinds of very complicated systems work together in order to make driving to the store so simple for me.

Someone had to figure out how an engine works and work with the folks who had figured out transmissions. There were the electrical engineers who worked with the chemical engineers to figure how to spark gasoline in my engine without torching the whole car. Speaking of gasoline, there were all the folks who had to figure *that* out, not to mention the folks who figured out rubber for my tires and the plastic that makes up most of the rest of my car.

You get the idea. Complex for them. Simple for me.

The same is true of seeking, recognizing and responding to what Jesus is already doing in the lives of people we are enjoying. Seeking, recognizing and responding to Jesus is simple for us. The *reason* it is simple for us is not so simple for Jesus. However, here's the point: Jesus can handle not-so-simple things very, very well.

I experienced this again one Saturday evening not long ago. Some of our neighbors down the block put out a last-minute invitation to join them in their driveway. They were frying up some gulf shrimp and wanted us to help them eat it. Being a dedicated neighborhood missionary, I was in.

My wife and I grabbed a bottle of wine and joined our neighbors in this impromptu gathering. We enjoyed hot fried shrimp and a chilled glass of white wine. It was fantastic! As we were standing there enjoying our friends (I will tell you the story of how we all became friends in chapter seventeen ... it was not very hard but it was very intentional), I started a conversation with Jim (not his real name). It started out with the usual, "Hey, how've you been doing?" However, within a few moments Jim wanted us to head off to the side to talk a little more privately.

In my mind I started asking, "Jesus, what are you up to here?"

Jim wanted to talk about his job. Ever since the sale of the company about a year ago things had been getting rough at work ... real rough. As he is telling me about the stress he is under and how this has been getting systematically worse in the last several weeks, it wasn't that tricky for me to recognize where some hope and redemption was needed in my friend's life. And wherever hope and redemption are needed, you can be sure of this: Jesus is present and working nearby. In other words, the kingdom of God is near.

So, Jim is standing there giving me a pretty good idea of where Jesus is working in his life. Now, the question is, "How can I join Jesus in what he is doing here?" It wasn't that complicated to find out. I just kept asking the next question. "So who do you know that can help you with getting a new job?" I asked. "It's not that simple," he replied. "I can't afford to start over again on the bottom rung of the pay scale."

"So what will you do?" I asked. "I don't *know*, Greg. I'm at a loss." His voice was reflecting his growing anxiety. "Have you invited God into it?" I asked.

Silence.

"No. No, I haven't," he replied. "Do you think it would help?"

"You mean, getting God involved? Yeah," I said with a smile, "I think that would help."

Then his kid fell over on a toy and scraped his elbow. So that's where the conversation ended. About 30 minutes later as I was enjoying yet another shrimp, his wife came up to me and said, "I don't know what you said to my husband, but he seems happier than I have seen him in a long time."

"It might be these really good shrimp," I said. "No, it wasn't the shrimp," she assured me, "And thank you."

But I hadn't really done anything. It was Jesus who was up to something with Jim. I had just been looking for what Jesus might choose to show me. Jesus did all the complex work. It was Jesus who worked out the precise timing of Jim and me standing together at an impromptu party eating really good shrimp. And it was only Jesus who could redeem trouble at the job to do something deeper in Jim's life. Jesus was messing with Jim redemptively, calling Jim back to himself.

All I did was point out the obvious. I couldn't *make* Jim turn to Jesus. But when Jim was *ready* to turn to Jesus, he found the peace and hope that Jesus had been offering him all along. I was just there to help.

Simple for me. Complex for Jesus. But Jesus handles complexity very, very well.

So, to summarize, in order to join Jesus on his redemptive mission that night all I had to do was

- Enjoy people by eating really good shrimp with them and hanging out;

- Seek what Jesus was already doing;

- Recognize what Jesus was already doing in Jim's life by listening to his story and realizing he was struggling with his job (which was really pretty obvious);

- And then respond to what Jesus was already doing in Jim's life by asking a couple questions and pointing out a simple spiritual truth.

Simple enough.

I couldn't manufacture this opportunity or control the result. All I could do was enjoy being with Jim, and then seek, recognize and respond to what Jesus was already doing in Jim's life. Jesus took care of all the complicated stuff.

Now let's take a few moments to unpack the theology behind all of this. Frankly, this is the kind of subject that deserves a slow, unhurried conversation on my front porch. With a comfortable breeze and something cool to sip we could unpack what Jesus taught story by story. Unfortunately we have to settle for a few pages in a book instead. But if you're ever in my neighborhood ...

We can begin by summarizing the theology this way:

> *The kingdom of God* (that is, the redemptive presence and activity of God in human lives) has come into the world to work out *the mission of God* (the redeeming and restoring of human lives to the kingdom of God) through *the people of God* (the redemptive presence and activity of God made tangible to other human beings).

My car has several complex systems working together in order to allow me to drive to the store simply. In the same way, God has his complex "systems" (namely, his kingdom and his mission) working together in order to allow us (his people) to be included in his redemptive mission ... and in a way that is simple enough for any of us to participate.

Let's take a look at each of these in turn: the kingdom of God, the mission of God and the people of God.

HERE'S THE POINT:

How do we seek, recognize and respond to what Jesus is already doing in the lives of the people we are enjoying? We start by paying attention to what he is already showing us. He says, "Open your eyes and look," for a reason.

CHAPTER 8
THE KINGDOM OF GOD

"What shall we say the kingdom of God is like?"

—Jesus in Mark 4:30

The mission of God is to redeem and restore all people to himself and is ignited and unleashed by the arrival of the kingdom of God into the created world first through Jesus and now through us.

Huh?

I know. Let's start unpacking this with an overview of what Jesus teaches us about the kingdom of God.

The kingdom of God is what Jesus came to announce, display and open up to all who would receive it.

Jesus indicates that the kingdom of God is already coming into our community each day and yet will not come in fullness until the last day. Jesus wants us to know that the kingdom is in play all around us, even though we may not get a direct look at it with our eyes. And yet Jesus still speaks of the kingdom as a present and redemptive reality that we can seek and find (Matthew 7:7). It is among us (Luke 17:21). It is within reach of us (Mark 12:34). It is messing with us (Matthew 13:33).

With the arrival of Jesus who is the king, the invisible kingdom of heaven is now coming into the created realm of earth ... breaking in ...

taking root ... taking over (Mark 3:27). The work of this kingdom is to reclaim and restore all created things (Revelation 21:5) but Jesus wants us to know that this "taking over" does not look like what the world would expect (Matthew 20:25). The restoration is taking root quietly (Mark 4:26-27) in the hearts of people (Mark 4:20), usually in little ways that can easily be underestimated (Matthew 13:31) but that will prove to be decisive and transforming in God's good time (Matthew 25:40).

And Jesus invites us to seek it first of all (Matthew 6:33).

When Jesus got himself born into our world, he brought his Father's kingdom with him. That means the kingdom is already in. Already happening. Already occurring right before our eyes. And we can see it if we seek it. In fact, Jesus says, the more we seek the more we will see (Matthew 7:8) and the more we see the more he can show us (Matthew 13:12). On the other hand, Jesus warns us that the kingdom can also be missed. Yes, it will be occurring right before our eyes, but will we recognize the activity we see as that of the kingdom (Luke 10:11)? Jesus warns us about being like so many who will "be ever seeing but never perceiving" (Matthew 13:14). In other words, there is a real danger that we will see what is, in fact, the activity of the kingdom of God right before our eyes but not recognize it (perceive it) as such. That's Jesus' warning. His *invitation* is for us to seek and recognize what is already happening, to watch for what is already occurring, to take note of what he is already doing in the lives of people around us.

And to join him.

Now, what does all this *mean*?

The announcement of the arrival of the kingdom of God is the stump speech of Jesus (Mark 1:15). It is what Jesus travels around teaching and displaying throughout the Gospels (Matthew 4:23). He uses the terms *kingdom, kingdom of God* and *kingdom of heaven* (all synonymous) over 100 times in the Gospels. If we are going to understand what Jesus was saying and doing in the Gospels, we need to understand what he meant by this term.

And what *does* he mean by it?

A working definition for us could be:

> The kingdom of God is the redemptive presence and activity of God in human lives.

To say it simply, the kingdom of God is God himself. Wherever God is present and active, his kingdom is present and active. So, in the beginning when God created the physical universe, and people particularly, we were created to live with God and be in a loving relationship with God (Genesis 1-2). And *living with God* is what especially the New Testament means by *living in the kingdom of God* (Colossians 1:13).

Unfortunately, by the third chapter of Genesis, this relationship was already broken and ruined by human beings through unfaithful rebellion (sin) and we were excluded from his kingdom.

So, what would God do?

He put into play a plan to redeem and restore the created universe, and people particularly, to himself – or, as the New Testament would say it, to his kingdom. This plan of redemption and restoration is the mission of God. However, until Jesus arrived into our world the kingdom of God would be out of reach for human beings. Thus, as we start working our way through the Old Testament, God's redemption and restoration of all things is a *promise* of what would come to pass *someday*. In the Old Testament the kingdom of God was most often described as being beyond us in the heavens or separated from us sinners in the Holy of Holies.

For instance, in Psalm 103:19 it says, "The LORD has established his throne in heaven, and his kingdom rules over all." At this point in the plan's timeline, the kingdom was described as the reign of God *over* us in the created world. This was an awesome proclamation. But because of our sin, it was also as fearsome to us as it was awesome (for example, think about Mt. Sinai in Exodus 19). At this point on the timeline of God's redemptive mission, the kingdom was awesome, fearsome and out of our reach.

However, in the New Testament, the Gospels begin announcing a new season in God's redemptive plan. It was a season that had been foretold from the beginning, but it was just now coming to pass in real time. The kingdom of God was now literally entering the created world through the incarnation of God himself in the man, Jesus of Nazareth. In other words, God got himself born into our created world in order to accomplish his own mission of redeeming and restoring all things to himself and to his kingdom.

John 1:14 describes in a straightforward way how God inaugurated this new season of redemption himself, "The Word [God] became flesh and made his dwelling among us." God got himself in. And, so, the promise of what God *would* do to redeem and restore his created world was what God was now *actually doing*. In other words, game-on! He no longer simply reigned *over* the created world fearsomely; he had now entered *into* the created world redemptively.

When Jesus then began his public ministry around the age of 30, his stump speech centered on this new season of redemption which he was launching. This stump speech is preserved for us in Mark 1:15, "The time has come. The kingdom of God is near. Repent and believe the good news!" What was perhaps most striking about Jesus' announcement of God's kingdom was that its coming was no longer fearsome to sinners (like it was on Mt. Sinai) but "good news" to sinners.

This "good news of the kingdom" is what Jesus went around unpacking in his teaching and displaying in his miracles (Matthew 4:23). This is what he discipled his followers to imitate and replicate (Mark 1:17, Luke 8:1, 9:1, 10:1, and Matthew 28:19-20). This "good news of the kingdom" excited and mobilized the outcast and marginalized while at the same time causing the religious elite to plot his murder. In the end, the reason Jesus' goal was to go to the cross was so that he could once and for all open the kingdom of God to all who would simply receive it – that is, receive the *full redemption and restoration of God*.

Good news, indeed.

It's all there in Jesus' stump speech. So, let's take a closer look at his announcement.

Jesus starts by saying, "*The time has come.*"

The word *time* is translated from the Greek word *kairos*. In Greek, there are two words commonly translated as *time*. One word is *chronos* which refers to the normal passing of time. This is the word which comes to us in the word *chronology*. But Jesus uses the other Greek word for time, *kairos*, which refers to an appointed time, a time anticipated and prepared for which is now here. What Jesus is saying is that the time for prophecies, promises and preparations is now complete. The season of waiting and hoping is over. The time has now arrived for fulfillment, for action and activation of the foretold season of redemption. From this time forward, everything will be different for our created world.

And what will be different from this time forward?

"The kingdom of God is near."

Jesus announces to all who would receive it that, from this moment forward, the kingdom of God is no longer unattainable to us up in the heavens or separated from us sinners behind the temple curtain in the Holy of Holies as it had been from of old. From now on, heaven has come to earth. There is now overlap. Intersection. Invasion. The kingdom has arrived. The kingdom has come and is now on the loose in our very midst. It is at hand, within reach, very near to each of us.

For what purpose? To begin what God had promised from the beginning: the reversal of what has become of the created world since its fall and ruin in Genesis 3. From the day of Adam, ruin had been spreading throughout the created world because of the rebellious activity of people. From now on, however, Jesus was putting into motion God's rescue mission of restoring people and making all things new as is celebrated in redemption's final triumph in Revelation 21.

And Jesus – standing in Galilee, making this announcement in Mark 1:15 – is literally the physical epicenter of this God-movement of restoration being unleashed. God's restoration arrived *in* Jesus and then got loose *through* Jesus. His restoration is not yet compete, but it is already spreading widely. Think of it like ripples on a pond that spread out from where a stone hits the water. The ripples have not yet reached the outer edges of the pond, but they are spreading and *will* reach the edges in due time. It is assured because the stone has already hit the water setting the ripples in motion. Think of it like a pinch of yeast that spreads out and permeates a loaf. The pinch of yeast has not yet reached throughout the loaf, but it is spreading and *will* reach throughout the loaf in due time. It is assured because the pinch of yeast has already been inserted into the loaf setting the yeast's permeation in motion.

In both instances, completion is assured, a done-deal, a slam-dunk because the stone has been thrown and the yeast has been inserted. It has started, it is happening, and it will be complete in due time.

So it is with God's rescue mission of redemption and restoration. From the moment Jesus threw the stone of his announcement in Galilee and then permanently inserted the yeast of redemption into the created world through his death and resurrection, completion was assured, a done-deal, a slam-dunk. God's restoration has not yet reached *throughout* the created world, but it has begun and is spreading and it *will* reach throughout the created world in due time. The ripples of restoration are going out to more and more people even now; the yeast of restoration is permeating more and more lives as we speak. All this was unleashed as Jesus launched his public ministry with the words, "The time has come. The kingdom of God is near."

In Luke 4:16-21 we are introduced to this same "unleashing" in another way. Jesus went to the synagogue in Nazareth and stood up to read a 700 year old prophecy from Isaiah. For 700 years the people of God had heard this prophecy. It recorded what God had promised to do; had committed to do; would *certainly* do ... someday.

Luke explains that when Jesus was handed the scroll, he found the passage he was looking for in Isaiah 61 and began to read it. "The Spirit of the LORD is on me," Jesus read, "because he has anointed me to preach good news to the poor. He has sent me to proclaim freedom for the prisoners and recovery of sight for the blind, to release the oppressed, to proclaim the year of the LORD's favor." This prophecy promised that someday God would unleash his redemption. Someday God would inaugurate the great reversal of the fall and ruin of his created world. Someday ...

Having finished reading what God had been promising for 700 years, Jesus rolls up the scroll, hands it back to the attendant and sits down. Luke records that the eyes of everyone in the room were fastened on Jesus. And that's when Jesus announces it: "Today ... *starting now* ... this scripture is fulfilled in your hearing."

In other words, *game-on*.

No more promising or waiting. From now on the words of Isaiah were unleashed and in play. From now on, Jesus said, redemption is on the loose. The full restoration of all things is in motion. The Spirit of God is on the move in the created world and will not be turned back until all things are made new.

"*From this time forward*," Jesus said to them, "*game-on*."

Luke and Mark end up in the same place. Mark 1:15, "*The time has come*," the time for waiting and hoping is complete. "*The kingdom of God is near*," from this time forward, the kingdom of God is in the world and in play. Game-on!

Which brings us to the final phrase Jesus uses in Mark 1:15. The phrase is intended to focus us on our response to his announcement: "*Repent and believe the good news*!" In other words, "What I want you to do in response to this announcement is repent and believe this good news!" When we hear the word *repent* we may think it means something like *stop doing naughty things*. And, indeed, we should stop doing naughty things. But the Greek word which is translated here as *repent* is the word *meta-noeo* which is much bigger than *stop doing naughty things*. Literally *meta-noeo* means a *changing of the mind* which is accompanied by a correspondingly *changed direction of life*.

In other words, Jesus is inviting us to completely reorient our minds and lives *around* this new reality of the kingdom being redemptively present and active around us. He is saying, "Reorient your thinking and presumptions around it. Reorient your values and priorities around it. Reorient how you interpret what you are seeing and hearing around it. And believe this good news I am telling you."

In chapter eleven I will show you how to do this in some very practical ways. But for now how does all this make joining Jesus on his mission simple for us? The pressure is off! Jesus doesn't send us to do these things *for* him; he invites us to come do these things *with* him. The kingdom has come and is on the move missionally. Jesus is already doing all the truly complicated work. All we have to do is enjoy the people he has put around us and pay attention to what Jesus might be up to in their lives.

It's called "seeking first the kingdom of God," (Matthew 6:33). We can do this.

Think of how your day could go tomorrow if you took up the practice of "seeking the kingdom." Tomorrow you will probably wake up and prepare for your day as usual. Perhaps you'll shower and have some breakfast. Hopefully you'll take some time to *meta-noeo* (reorient your mind) around the good news that the kingdom will be on the move around you today.

Then what?

As we walk out our front door and into the new day, we can have two simple questions on our mind: "Jesus, what are you up to today?" And then, "How would you have me join you?"

You see, as we head into our new day, we can have great confidence that the kingdom has already come and the missional presence and activity of Jesus is already in play. We don't have to worry about how to get Jesus into our offices, classrooms or neighborhoods. He's already on the move there. We don't have to concern ourselves with how Jesus will ripen people for their next-step toward faith. He's already on it.

All we really have to do is look for what Jesus is already showing us. In other words, seek the kingdom. Look for what is already happening.

And join in.

HERE'S THE POINT

The kingdom of God is God himself and came into the created world through Jesus. When Jesus arrived here, he unleashed the promised season of world redemption. It is happening now. Wherever God is redemptively present and active his kingdom is at work. We can seek it, recognize it and join with it.

CHAPTER 9
WHAT DOES THE KINGDOM OF GOD LOOK LIKE?

"Therefore every teacher ... who has been instructed about the kingdom of heaven is like the owner of a house who brings out of his storeroom new treasures as well as old."

— Jesus in Matthew 13:52

So, if we can seek and find the activity of the kingdom of God around us, the next question is, "What does it look like?"

Certainly God "shows" us his kingdom in various ways. For instance, whenever we go by a church building, we have a pretty good idea that the kingdom of God is near because wherever God's Word and sacraments are being offered, the kingdom of God is redemptively operational. That's simple enough to "see." Likewise, it's not too hard to "see" the kingdom's presence and activity when we see a person's "love, joy, peace, patience, kindness, goodness, faithfulness, gentleness and self-control," (Galatians 5:22-23). Paul calls this the fruit (or evidence) of the Spirit's presence and activity in a human life.

Jesus also says in John 13:35, "By this all men will know that you are my disciples, if you love one another." In other words, if you see a Jesus-follower loving others you are seeing and recognizing evidence that the kingdom is present and active through the person. Again, simple enough to "see."

However, what about everyone else? What does the kingdom of God look like when it is present and active in the life of someone living *without* the good news of the kingdom? When someone doesn't yet know, or understand or believe the kingdom has come and redemption is theirs? What does the kingdom look like when it is still ripening someone *toward* redemption?

It will usually look like human need. It will look like where love, hope or redemption are *needed*. We can look around and ask ourselves, "Where can grace be applied? Where can a little love and truth make a difference?"

For those living *within* the kingdom, love is the evidence of the redemption the kingdom has brought. For those living *without* the kingdom, human need is the evidence that the kingdom is near and working toward *bringing* redemption.

We learn to seek and recognize the kingdom in this way by watching Jesus in the Gospels. He recognizes the human need around him and begins to respond to it. Think about how often we see Jesus pressing in and coming near to those in need. There were those who had physical needs, like those who needed healing or food. But there were also those who had spiritual, emotional and relational needs as well.

- Nicodemus in John 3 asking the hard questions he was wrestling with
- The woman at the well in John 4 entangled in toxic relationships and religion
- The disciples in Matthew 18 arguing over who was the greatest

- The woman in Mark 5 suffering from both an issue of blood and the rejection of her community

- The crowds in Matthew 9 who were harassed and helpless but also ready for good news

- The man in Mark 9 who needed faith but could not yet muster faith

- The man in Mark 12 who had right answers but not yet right understanding

- The rich young ruler in Luke 18 who wavered between the kingdom and his stuff, the fulfilment he sought and the sadness for which he settled

- The woman caught in adultery in John 8 who very nearly threw her life away for fleeting pleasure

Human need. The places where redemption is still needed.

By seeing their various needs, Jesus recognized where the kingdom was at work in them and he recognized that they were actually ready for him to respond.

The bottom line is this: if we see a need for redemption and restoration in a human being, whatever it might be, we can recognize that the kingdom of God is nearby and active. Why? *Because that's where Jesus will be.* Remember, Jesus is on a mission. Redemption is what Jesus does. We don't have to wonder if he is ready to respond to the need. So we watch for what he is already showing us. "What is Jesus up to today? Where can grace be applied?" We can do this with strangers along life's way. But what if we regularly did this with people within our relational reach?

By the way, seeing what Jesus is showing us in our daily life is not done through magic or mysticism. It's done through the Gospels. By reading the Gospels over and over again, we can watch what Jesus has already shown us and listen to what Jesus has already told us. What Jesus did in the Gospels he is still doing today. What Jesus said in the Gospels he's still saying today. The more we watch and listen to Jesus in the Gospels the more we will recognize what we are seeing and hearing from him in our daily life.

"For everyone who seeks finds," Jesus says (Matthew 7:8). "He who has ears to hear, let him hear," (Mark 4:9).

Sometimes "seeking and finding" is easy. The need is obvious. The pain is clear. Like the beaten man lying on the road in the story of the Good Samaritan. If we came across such a man, we would literally have to step around the person to avoid him. However, because Jesus is showing the person to us, maybe instead of avoiding them, we could respond to them.

I was out cutting my lawn this last July during the hottest part of the day. Not smart in League City, Texas. So I was taking a water break in the shade of my garage trying to cool off. As I stood there, I noticed one of my neighbors walking by on the sidewalk in the hot summer sun. Folks don't usually do that in Texas. As she came closer I could see that she was noticeably upset. I knew this woman. She's one of my neighbors. Something was wrong. It was easy to recognize that the kingdom of God would be nearby. I was there. She was walking by with a lot on her mind.

Coincidence? I don't believe in coincidences any more. Only God-incidences. So I called out to her.

She was a little startled to realize someone was nearby. She hadn't noticed me. She was also a little embarrassed to be discovered in her angst. However, God knew how this needed to go. The details are not important. Suffice it to say that she needed someone to ask how she was doing and to be willing to listen. We ended with a prayer on the sidewalk and some hope.

"Seeing" the kingdom was pretty simple in that case.

Often it is not as obvious. Most of us have become very good at keeping our hearts hidden. People make it hard for us to see what is actually going on inside of them. (I know I can be pretty good at hiding my heart ... how about you?) However, if we continue to be with people, and enjoy them as we are seeking and listening, eventually even those who are good at hiding will show us where Jesus is at work in their life.

During my college summers, I worked for an offshore drilling company. Oil companies hired us to drill their oil wells. After we drilled the hole, they came in and started pumping the oil. One summer, the drilling business wasn't doing very well. Instead of our rig being in Alaska or the Gulf of Mexico drilling, it was sitting idle in the mouth of the Sabine River. We had a skeletal crew on the rig that summer, just enough people to keep it maintained and to protect it from anyone who might want to walk off with some free scrap metal.

The rig boss announced he needed a couple crew members to work the night shift. Whoever was chosen wouldn't need to do much maintenance. Mostly they needed to guard the rig from bad guys coming on board. Since I am such a big strong menacing man (this is said with a sarcastic tone), I was somehow chosen to be one of the two night watchmen.

The other man was Joe. Joe really was a big strong menacing man.

We looked like a comedy team—only it wasn't funny. He was about six feet, four inches tall and weighed about 230 pounds. He never smiled. Ever.

I was maybe five foot, ten inches tall with my boots on and weighed about 160 pounds right after a really big meal. And I smiled. A lot. Especially when I got nervous.

Back then I wouldn't have had the vocabulary to describe it this way, but the "kingdom of God" was definitely up to something by putting Joe and me together that summer.

Joe was angry, harsh, bitter, cynical and ... did I mention he was angry?

And I got to spend 12 hours every night with Joe drinking coffee and hearing what he was angry about. At first I just tried to endure it. Then I started listening more carefully. Behind all the sarcasm and cynicism and foul language was a lot of hurt. Eventually, I figured something out. Joe was a person. And in between all of Joe's harsh words and attitudes was a guy wondering if there was any hope, any justice, any way to somehow get past the grinding disappointments he had endured.

Joe was absolutely not interested in anything having to do with church or religion. Of course, after I heard some of his stories, I couldn't blame him. If what had happened to him had happened to me, I would be angry and cynical, too. Over time, Joe found out I was someone who followed Jesus. And while, at first, that was a target for some of his church-focused anger, eventually I was able to help him untangle the difference between Jesus and what he had experienced at the hands of church people. I never did make much progress with Joe on the subject of church, but he did start asking more questions about Jesus.

Very early on, I realized that I couldn't fix Joe and that he didn't want fixing. But as I simply watched and listened, (again, I didn't have this vocabulary back then) I realized the kingdom of God was nearby and active around Joe's anger, swagger and pain.

Joe and I became friends that summer. He still could be gruff and still shot profanity at me whenever he was complaining about my various shortcomings. But the deepest pain Joe had been carrying around seemed to diminish. Peace occasionally showed itself on his face as we talked about God's grace and about better ways to live in a messed up world. And from time to time Joe even smiled. It wasn't pretty but at least it was a smile.

I never saw Joe again after that summer. I don't know if he ever came to trust Jesus or not. I know that by the end of that summer, he still hadn't. However, I also know that the kingdom intersected Joe's life that summer in a way that began its redemptive work in him. The work wasn't complete, but the stone was thrown. The yeast was inserted. The kingdom had come to Joe and started him on his journey of redemption and restoration.

All I had to do was notice.

And join in. That's why joining Jesus on his mission is simple for us.

"What's Jesus up to today? Where can grace be applied?"

HERE'S THE POINT

If we see a need in a human being we can recognize that the kingdom of God is nearby and active. That is what Jesus invites us to look for, recognize and respond to.

CHAPTER 10
THE MISSION OF GOD

"That is why I have come."

—Jesus in Mark 1:38

And what *is* Jesus up to today? The question is a "kingdom of God" question. It is about noticing how the kingdom is coming now, in this moment, in the lives of people around us. "What is Jesus showing me? What is he inviting me to notice? What is he up to here?" The ultimate answer to the question, of course, is that Jesus is up to the mission of God. And what is "the mission of God?" By now the following working definition will seem familiar:

> The mission of God is to redeem and restore all things to the Kingdom of God, beginning with human beings.

We cannot redeem and restore people to the Father's kingdom. That is the job of Jesus. Our job is to see who is ripe for his redemption. As Jesus says in John 4:35 all we have to do is, "Open your eyes and look at the fields. They are ripe for harvest." Ripe means ready. So, what is Jesus inviting us to open our eyes and see? What is Jesus showing us? What does Jesus want us to notice?

People. People who are ready.

"Open your eyes and look." Who is ready for some news that is good? Who is ready for a little hope, a little help, a little grace? Who is ready for a cool cup of water of truth? In Jesus, the kingdom of God has come into the world to work out the mission of God. The only question left is *how*?

And that brings us to us.

We have now finally come to our simple role in Jesus' redemptive mission. N.T. Wright, an Anglican bishop and leading New Testament scholar, writes, "We're called, here and now, to be instruments of God's new creation which has already launched in Jesus and of which Jesus' followers are supposed to be not simply beneficiaries *but also agents*," (emphasis mine). We are beneficiaries but also agents of God restoring his created world. This is our simple but important role in his plan. We are the *how* of Jesus' redemptive mission getting released into the material world of human beings. Paul explains it by calling the people of God "the body of Christ." He writes in 1 Corinthians 12:27, "Now you are the body of Christ, and each one of you is a part of it." Being "the body of Christ" is not simply a theological metaphor Paul utilizes. It is a statement of fact. Because the Spirit of Jesus lives in us, we are literally the visible body of the invisible Jesus to the people around us.

"Don't you know that you yourselves are God's temple and that God's Spirit lives in you?" (1 Corinthians 3:16).

We are Jesus with skin on. We are a tangible glove for his intangible hand. We are *how* people experience Jesus. Through our hands people experience the hands of Jesus. Through our voice people hear the voice of Jesus. Through our service people experience the care of Jesus. Through our face people see the face of Jesus.

Jesus brings himself to people *through* us.

Paul explains it this way in Galatians 2:20, "I have been crucified with Christ and I no longer live, but Christ lives in me. The life I now live in the body, I live by faith in the Son of God, who loved me and gave himself for me." Or to put it another way, the life I am now physically living in this tangible body is for the sake of others being able to see and experience the invisible person of Jesus *through* me. As the people of God, we are the visible, tangible contact points between the kingdom which is real but spiritual and the created world which is real but physical. We are the way the kingdom-on-mission breaks into the flesh-and-blood-world of human beings and has its effect. In other words, it's the kingdom's work, but it comes to human beings through us.

From the kingdom, *through* us.

Remember Joe, my oil rig friend? Before I was teamed with Joe for the nightshift, was Jesus present for Joe? Was the kingdom of God there for Joe? Were the love of God and the redemptive plan of God immediately available to Joe in his pain? Of course.

But Joe didn't know that. He had no way of seeing Jesus or hearing Jesus or experiencing Jesus in his earthly life. Joe only had access to the created world of human beings. And that was broken. A physical contact point was needed between Jesus' invisible presence and the visible world of Joe. Jesus had to become tangible so that Joe could encounter him.

So God put me on the nightshift.

I couldn't redeem and restore Joe. That was Jesus' work. I was 20 years old and didn't have a clue about how to bring healing and restoration to a big, mean man like Joe. All I could do was show up for my shift and be who I already was, a person in whom Jesus lived and through whom Jesus gradually made himself known to Joe.

From Jesus, *through* me.

It wasn't me; it was Christ living through me. Like Paul and you, I have been crucified with Christ, and I no longer live, but Christ lives in me. The life I now live in the body, I live by faith in the Son of God, who loved me and gave himself for me. So a working definition for "the people of God" could be the following:

> Those who bear the Spirit of God are the redemptive presence and activity of God made tangible to other human beings.

And how does the kingdom become tangible through us? Jesus says it's through little things. Jesus says the kingdom coming is like a little seed, a pinch of yeast or a cool cup of water. It comes through a little food for the hungry, a little time for the isolated, a little hope for the least of these.

In American Christianity, too often we think we have to do something big for Jesus in order for it to count. We feel like we need to try to hit a home run for Jesus! We can certainly try to do big things for Jesus. We can try to fill big stadiums with thousands of worshippers. We can try to build big programs with big budgets to fund them. We can attempt hard things, amazing things, things the history books will record.

But Jesus doesn't seem to point to such things in the Gospels.

When Jesus shows us how to join his mission he points to little things, things that are within our reach, things that may not be noticed by thousands of people but will make a difference to one. A little love, a little joy, a little truth, a little patience. Jesus says that through little things such as these, the kingdom comes and the will of the Father is done here on earth as it is in heaven. Through the little seed comes the large result. Through the little pinch of yeast comes the taking-over of the whole. Through the cool cup of water comes the quenching of the thirst for God.

Do you want to hit a home run for Jesus today? Try responding to the simple little opportunities he invites you to notice. Are you afraid you won't be able to hit a home run for Jesus today? Try responding to the simple little opportunities he invites you to notice. And *through* your response, the presence of Jesus will become real to that person.

From Jesus, *through* us.

We are the presence of Jesus made tangible in our families, neighborhoods, workplaces and schools. The love we show, the patience we have, the notice we take, the attention we give, the truth we speak, the hope we inspire is not us but Christ living in and through us.

This is why our participation in the mission of Jesus is simple.

We can do this.

Recently, Susan and I were leading a missional training and we asked, "What scares you as you think of yourself as a missionary?" The answers were predictable. God's people everywhere seem to feel the same way. "What scares me?" one man replied, "Failure. Rejection. Embarrassment. That I will mess up God's work. Other than that, not much." Can you relate? The good news is that Jesus isn't counting on us being perfect missionaries. He knows we mess up. In fact, he's counting on it. He knows that even the simplest aspects of living missionally will get away from us sometimes. We get distracted. We get selfish. We stop watching. We stop responding when Jesus tees it up for us with a person he has been preparing.

We blow it.

We fail.

Now what?!

Do you have a GPS? One of those devices that gives you directions for getting from point A to point B in the car? What happens when you miss a turn? It told you to turn. It prompted you to turn in plenty of time for you to make the turn. You just got distracted for a moment or a little confused or you didn't quite trust the GPS ... whatever the case, you missed the turn.

What happens then? Failure? Embarrassment? Condemnation?

"Recalculating."

No matter how lost or far off course we end up, the GPS knows how to get us where we need to go. GPS's were set up for imperfect people like us. Jesus knows we're imperfect, too. He is prepared for this. He knows how to work all things according to his purpose. When we miss our missional opportunity, when we blow by our missional turn, we repent and he recalculates. We may not be very good at being missionaries, but he is *very* good at being God.

He's got this.

HERE'S THE POINT

Jesus is already doing everything necessary to make our participation in his mission simple. All we have to do is reorient our minds to his good news and keep asking Jesus two questions: What are you up to? And how would you have me join you?

CHAPTER 11
GETTING INTO POSITION
EVERY DAY

"Wherever you go, there you are."

—Winnie-the-Pooh

J esus is very clever. Wherever he wants you to start being a missionary, he already has you there. Whoever he wants you to love and serve redemptively, he already has you in their proximity. As the great theologian Winnie-the-Pooh once observed, "Wherever you go, there you are." To which I would simply add, "And wherever you are, Jesus is already working redemptively." As we have seen in the first part of this book, the question is not, "Is Jesus up to something in the lives of people around me?" Rather, the question is, *"What* is Jesus up to?" And, "How is he inviting me to *join him*?" This is our missional mindset.

Only Jesus can do the Jesus-work of redeeming and restoring people to the Kingdom of the Father he loves. However, he invites us to join him by enjoying the people he has put in our proximity and then seeking, recognizing and responding to what he is already doing in their lives. The second part of this book focuses on *how* we do that. The *how* of missional living begins with something Dwelling 1:14 calls the "5 Practices." We advocate the 5 Practices because they help mission-minded people like you be in position to join Jesus every day in simple, practical ways. What are these five mission practices?

1. Seeking the Kingdom

2. Hearing from Jesus

3. Talking with People

4. Doing Good

5. Ministering through Prayer

We will unpack each of the 5 Practices in the next several chapters. However, before we do let's frame our conversation so we will be on the same page.

First, the 5 Practices were chosen for the practical reason that when we put them into play, they do an effective job of positioning us to enjoy people and to seek, recognize and respond to what Jesus is already doing in the lives of the people we are enjoying. The 5 Practices should not be seen as an exhaustive list of godly practices. God's people have found many practices to be helpful over the centuries. However, the 5 Practices are particularly good at positioning us for the daily life of being a missionary. In fact, Susan and I "discovered" the effectiveness of these simple practices on the foreign mission trips we took. When we were in a foreign mission field, our teams would gather every morning to hear from Jesus in his Word and be reminded that he was going to be out there on the loose that day. Then, after the day was completed, we gathered together to report back to each other what we had seen God doing and how we were able to be a part of it. After a few years of mission trips it finally dawned on us that we could put these missional practices into play every day, not just when we were on foreign mission trips.

Bottom line: The 5 Practices work wherever we go – across the world or across the street – because they put us into position to join with what Jesus is already doing in the lives of the people around us.

Second, the 5 Practices are not part of a church program; they are part of a daily lifestyle. This is not about adding a mission program to the other programs at your church. We are not suggesting you find time on the busy church calendar to gather in the Fellowship Hall once a month to do the 5 Practices. The 5 Practices are not what we do when we *go* to church. The 5 Practices are what we do when we go out to *be* the Church and join Jesus in our everyday lives. They are a simple set of practices we can put into play as part of our daily comings and goings – wherever we are and whoever we are with – in order to be in position to join Jesus on a moment's notice. Remember, Jesus is on the move every day. You just never know what he may be up to. So we put the 5 Practices into play so that whenever it is Jesus' time to break into the life of a person nearby, we are in position to notice and join him.

I recently was copied on a string of emails between a man named Les, who lives in the inner city of Edmonton, Alberta, Canada and a young pastor named Matt. Pastor Matt also lives in the inner city but pastors a church in the suburbs of Edmonton. I've had the privilege of working with Matt as he seeks to figure out how to join Jesus' mission in his inner city neighborhood. Soon I will be working with the people in his congregation, too, who want to do the same in their suburban neighborhoods. Les' email below was sparked by Matt's recent invitation to come to the first missional training that we as Dwelling 1:14 would provide.

Les wrote:

"Matt, Read with interest the email about Greg Finke, Kingdom Seeking and the Dwelling 1:14 training, and this question immediately came to mind, 'Do you think this approach would have an application in the inner city?' You do not know me and so the following is a short explanation of why I ask this question. My wife Emily and I have been attending Bethel [Matt's large suburban congregation] for about seven months. We have been living and serving in the city in various ministries since 1996. During this time Emily has been teacher and principal of our neighbourhood school, as well. Recently, I have been serving at The Rock [an inner city ministry in Edmonton], and this past May was asked to join its board. The question has been on my mind: what would it take to make a difference – especially spiritually – in the lives of the people who come through the doors each week? Therefore, my original question above. Hopefully Greg's approach offers some help for the inner city as well as the suburbs, however if this training is strictly for Bethel and outreach in Sherwood Park [the suburb] please let me know."

To which Matt responded:

"Hi Les! This isn't a program in the sense of where these things would 'work.' It's about being a follower of Jesus in your neighbourhood or wherever you find yourself – at work, The Rock, even at church! :) The kingdom exists wherever we live and move and have our being. I just seem to miss it sometimes. I think the Dwelling 1:14 approach would be beneficial anywhere it's followed – mainly because Jesus is on the loose, out of the grave and he's doing his work before any of us ever arrive on the scene. In fact, this approach of watching where Jesus is at work has opened doors for me with my neighbours – my family and I live in the city, too. I won't share the whole story here but eventually my neighbor (who didn't know I go to church or that I'm a pastor) asked me if I'd teach him what's in the Bible because he's never read it and never been to church. This only happened because, over time, he got to know me and trusted me. I got to pray for him and talk with him and entrust him to God's care. A God who has other people who will connect with my neighbour in other ways. In the end, I think Greg would remind us that God is an incarnational God who connects with us relationally. And we're to do the same in the power of his Spirit. I'm still learning how to do this and to trust that I'm truly invited to do this in little ways (and sometimes big ways that only appear little). Hope that helps a bit. I'll Cc this to my friend (and your future friend) Greg."

To which I finally replied:

"Matt and Les: Yes, Matt, you pretty much nailed it. Wherever people are - inner city, suburbs, rural - Jesus is there loving, interacting and redeeming them. He invites us to be there, too, with the people, watching and responding to what Jesus is doing redemptively in their lives. I have worked with many people who are living and ministering in inner cities... Baltimore, St. Louis, Minneapolis, San Diego, and New Orleans come to mind. If Jesus is there, we, his people, can join him and be a part of his redemptive mission. Dwelling 1:14 is not about a program, it is about a missional lifestyle focused on joining Jesus wherever he invites us in. Hope to meet you soon, Les!"

So, where has Jesus already put you? And with whom has he already put you?

HERE'S THE POINT

Are you ready to move beyond an occasional mission program and become an everyday missionary? Then let's get in position with the 5 Practices.

CHAPTER 12
SEEKING THE KINGDOM

"Seek first the kingdom of God ..."

—Jesus in Matthew 6:33

J esus has brought the kingdom of God into our world and into our community. Therefore, the practice of "seeking the kingdom" is the first practical step we can take in joining Jesus in what he is doing. The more we seek the more Jesus can show us; and the more we seek the more Jesus can do with us. So, what is Jesus already showing us? What is he already inviting us to notice and do?

John the Baptist reminds us that we can only act on what God is giving. He said concerning his ministry, "A man can receive only what is given him from heaven" (John 3:27). His words apply to seeking the kingdom of heaven in general. We don't have to manipulate or cajole kingdom opportunities. We watch for them. Isn't it good to know we don't have to manufacture kingdom opportunities? That's God's job. Proverbs 16:9 says it concisely, "In his heart a man plans his course, but the LORD determines his steps." So the pressure is off us. We go about our day as planned but we watch for what Jesus is up to in the midst of it.

Are you sometimes irritated by the people who interrupt your day? I know I can be. Maybe now is a good time to stop seeing such moments as interruptions and start seeing them as appointments ...

appointments set up by God without consulting with us. "In his heart a man plans his course, but the LORD determines his steps." If we believe Jesus when he says his kingdom is in the world and on the move around us, it changes how we perceive what is going on around us ... or it could.

Wherever you go, there you are, and wherever you are, Jesus is already up to something. Therefore, coincidences become God-incidences. Good luck becomes God's anonymous provision. Bad luck becomes God's redirection of our plans. The human needs we see in our neighbors, co-workers and friends no longer can be set aside and ignored (like the priest and Levite do in the story of the Good Samaritan) but now are personal invitations from Jesus for us to *respond* (like the Samaritan who stepped in and not around when he saw the man on the road).

One word of caution: we may not always discern accurately how God wants us to understand what we are seeing. Seeking and recognizing the kingdom is not an invitation to be impetuous in response. I don't know about you, but if I am not careful, I can see what God is showing me and then jump to a wrong conclusion. It is one thing to respond in the moment to an obvious opportunity to be kind or offer service to a neighbor. It is another when we believe the response might be a crossroad for our life. For this reason, we advocate the missional community. We will unpack what a missional community is in chapter 19. However, suffice it to say that in times which require wisdom and discernment it is good to have a community of fellow missionaries to help us process what God is asking of us.

For example, one of the young couples in our missional community had been taking up the first practice of seeking the kingdom. Because of that, they had a growing sense God was asking them to leave their gated, suburban apartment complex to move into one of the poorest parts of the city. This was not a decision to be made impetuously. Clearly, God had been showing them things, but we wanted to help them sort through what they were seeing and get clear confirmation he was asking them to make this life-changing move.

As it turned out, the evidence became overwhelming that God was asking them to do this. They were seeking and they were finding. And so they made preparations to move. When the day came for us to help them move out of their apartment and into the city, we were able to do it with joy and not trepidation. We kept seeking and he kept showing us things until we had no choice but to gladly obey.

HERE'S THE POINT

The practice of seeking the kingdom is simply forming the habit of watching for what God is showing us every day in the midst our daily routines. How have you seen God at work in your life this week?

CHAPTER 13
HEARING FROM JESUS

"This is my beloved Son ... Listen to him!"

—God the Father speaking of God the Son in Matthew 17:5

The second practice is hearing from Jesus. When we say, "Hearing from Jesus," we are not claiming to hear from Jesus mystically but through the clear (and challenging) words of the Gospels. What Jesus said in the Gospels he is still saying today. And what Jesus did in the Gospels he is still doing today. If we want to recognize what Jesus is telling us or showing us in our daily lives, it begins with us being deeply familiar with what he's already shown us and told us in the Gospels.

For this reason, several years ago, I began a personal quest to get to know Jesus better. I found the best way to do that is to open the Gospels and simply join the crowds following Jesus around, listening to what he actually said, watching what he actually did and really wrestling with what he means. Essentially, I allowed Jesus to mess with me like he did his first disciples – to stretch me and invite me to believe more and do more.

There's no one correct way to get into the Gospels. And there's no easy way to wrestle with Jesus. But here are some tips:

1. The early morning is a good time to listen to Jesus in the Gospels. The habit of Jesus was to get up early to go listen to his Father (see Mark 1:35). As Jesus-followers it might not

be a bad idea to imitate him in this practice. As someone once said, "It is better to tune your instrument before the concert begins rather than after it has concluded." Good point.

2.   As you prepare to open the Gospels, invite the Holy Spirit to open your eyes, ears and heart to what Jesus is going to give you today. After all, this is a spiritual endeavor empowered by the Spirit. By the way, while devotional materials can be very helpful for gaining insight into Jesus' teachings, try to avoid consistently substituting devotional materials for actually reading and wrestling with the words of Jesus yourself. In some ways, reading devotional materials is like having someone else physically work out for you. It's easier, but doesn't do you nearly as much good as when you work out yourself.

3.   Don't read to get through the words of Jesus. Read to get the words of Jesus through you. Take your time. You may only get through a couple verses. Let the Spirit of Jesus bless you, wrestle with you, show you things, and invite you to do things as you go out into your day.

4.   Don't settle for simply "studying about" what Jesus did and said. Let it be about talking with him and coming to understand how you are to put his words into practice. You can do that by asking Jesus this simple question: What would you have me believe and do as a result of your words today?

Jesus says this directly in Matthew 7:24-27, "Therefore everyone who hears these words of mine and puts them into practice is like a wise man who built his house on the rock ... But everyone who hears these words of mine and does not put them into practice is like a foolish man who built his house on sand ..." Jesus wants us to move beyond hearing and studying his words to putting them into practice. Putting his words into practice is not about proving ourselves to be good Christians. Putting his words into practice is about us finding out what happens when we put the teachings of Jesus into play in the real world.

In Matthew 7, Jesus is moving us beyond information (hearing his words) to transformation (finding out what happens when we put them into practice). Finding out what *actually* happens when we put the teachings of Jesus into practice *transforms* us. This is what Jesus means when he says the wise person is on the rock and the foolish one is on the sand. One is changed and the other is not. What makes one wise and the other foolish? What makes one be on rock and the other be on sand? Both hear the words of Jesus. The difference? One puts the words into practice and is changed by what he finds out and the other does not.

Studying the words of Jesus is good, but he wants us to move on to *doing* them. In other words, he wants us to move on from "Bible study" to "Bible doing." When we put the words of Jesus into practice, we find out stuff about Jesus and his kingdom. As a result of finding out, we become wiser and experienced in matters of the kingdom. We now *know* what to expect when we put the words of Jesus into play in real life. We've actually done it. Such knowledge is no longer simply theoretical for us, it is now experiential. We now know what happens because we have actually put his words into play. This increases our wisdom of how the kingdom actually works in the world but it also increases our confidence in Jesus. The more we put his words and practices into play the more confidence we gain in *him*. It feels more and more like we are standing on rock rather than sand.

Are you unsure about the veracity of what Jesus says about how the kingdom operates in the rough and rugged world of your everyday life? It may be time to stop settling for hearing his words and start taking the risk of putting them into play.

HERE'S THE POINT

The practice of hearing from Jesus in the Gospels is all about being able to better recognize and respond to what Jesus is telling and showing us on our daily mission trip in everyday life. What has he been teaching you in his Word lately?

CHAPTER 14
TALKING WITH PEOPLE

"It's hard not to like someone once you know their story."
—Fred Rogers of "Mr. Rogers' Neighborhood"

Jesus can do more with two people who are talking with each other than he can with two people who are successfully ignoring each other.

Think about how many people are regularly within our proximity. Same people, same place, same time, week after week. Do we take the opportunity to notice them or do we look past them? There are neighbors we've never met. There are coworkers we've never thought of beyond work logistics. We've had the same cashier or wait staff or UPS person serve us time after time but never took time to get their name. How often have we successfully ignored the other parents waiting with us for our children to get out of music lessons or sports practices? We look straight ahead pretending no one is there. And our culture would call that normal. But what if that began to change?

First, we need to start noticing the people God has regularly placed in proximity to us. Who is already there?

I met Cindy at a Dwelling 1:14 training. As the group discussed this practice of noticing and talking with people, she realized something. Later, Cindy came up to me and sheepishly told me that she went to the same sandwich shop and ordered the same sandwich from the same young lady behind the counter nearly every day. In fact, Cindy was so regular in this habit that when the young lady behind the counter saw Cindy driving up, she began making the sandwich she knew Cindy would order! And what did Cindy realize about this? After all those encounters with the young lady, not once had Cindy asked her for her name. She had successfully ignored her. She hadn't meant to. She just hadn't thought of the sandwich shop as a potential spot for the kingdom of God to show up. (Cindy was embarrassed by this realization and resolved to take the simple step of introducing herself the next time she was there.)

A young man I met at this same training had a similar realization. Every morning he took his dog out for a walk. At a certain point along the way, most every day there was a maintenance worker hunched over a control box of some kind. This control box was right by the sidewalk so nearly every day our young friend had to literally squeeze by the maintenance worker to continue on his way. The young man realized that he had been successfully ignoring a person God was putting right in front of him day after day! He hadn't meant to. He just hadn't thought a maintenance worker might be someone Jesus wanted him to meet. Our young friend resolved to change that the next time he saw the man. It could be as simple as saying, "Good morning! You know, I feel kind of silly walking around you every morning without knowing your name. Hi, I'm ..." From there, you just never know what might happen.

But this much is clear: Jesus can do more with two people who are talking with each other than he can with two people who are successfully ignoring each other. After we start being more intentional about noticing the people God has regularly placed in our proximity, it also becomes easier to start a conversation with them. After all, you are regularly showing up in the same place. So start simply. Ask them their name. In time, as encounter builds on encounter and conversation builds on conversation, you begin to find out who they are, where they're from, what their story is, and what matters to them. And they will learn these things about you, too. It's called "friendship." But remember, since these are people we will see on a fairly regular basis we don't have to be in a hurry.

On the other hand, perhaps you are one of the many people who are uncomfortable talking with people you don't know. I've got good news. Turns out, talking with people is less about *talking* than it is about *listening*. After all, we describe this practice as "Talking *with* People." That means we talk but mostly we listen. Will Rogers once expressed it this way, "I never learned anything while I was talking." I guess, come to think of it, neither have I.

When I first became more intentional about noticing and talking with people around me, I was surprised by how many people, given the chance, would open up and begin sharing their story with me even though they didn't know me very well. I wouldn't pry, I was just available. I would simply listen and ask the next question. Almost like I was interviewing them. It wasn't hard because I genuinely took interest in what they were telling me. Over the years, I have ended up having many great conversations with people in this same way. It's almost as if these dear people *needed* someone to talk with.

And do you know what? They do.

Survey after survey shows that Americans are among the most lonely and isolated people on earth. We live in crowded cities but are largely on our own. The American Sociological Review recently reported that 53% of Americans have no one (outside of their immediate family) with whom they can discuss important matters. In other words, more than half the people we see every day have almost no one who gives a rip about what they are thinking, wondering or wresting with.

What if we did?

"When Jesus saw the crowds, he had compassion on them ..." (Matthew 9:36). What if we really started "seeing" those in the crowd around us like Jesus did? What if we started seeing these people with compassion? What if we remembered our simple axiom that Jesus can do more with two people who have started talking with each other than he can with two people who are successfully ignoring each other?

Does talking with people guarantee something spiritual will happen? No. But *not* talking with people guarantees that it won't happen.

One last thought. Is this practice of talking with people for extroverts or introverts? It's an important question because roughly half of us are extroverts and half of us are introverts. If living missionally is only for extroverts, and, therefore, only half of us have a role to play in the mission, Jesus has a flawed strategy. The answer, of course, is that the missional practice of talking with people is for extroverts *and* introverts. God has wired some of us to be introverts and some of us to be extroverts for a reason. God intends that we interact with people at the relational pace with which he has wired us. If God made you an introvert he just might want you to proceed at an introvert's pace.

The truth is extroverts and introverts bring both strengths and weakness to the practice. Extroverts are good at initiating and talking, but they are not as good at listening and asking the next question. On the other hand, introverts are good at noticing and watching people, but struggle to initiate conversation. However, once the conversation is initiated, introverts often excel at listening. In fact, a strong argument can be made that introverts are actually better suited for missional conversation – once the difficulty of initiating conversation is overcome – because they would rather ask questions and listen than hear themselves talking.

Recently I was doing a missional training in the Chicago area. During the meal break I was sitting with a man who was excited to tell me his local mission stories. He admitted that he had not had much success during his earlier years, even though he was an extrovert. I asked him what had changed. He laughed and said, "God could do more with me when I finally learned to shut my mouth and start listening to what people were telling me." I laughed with him because I completely understood. I'm an extrovert, too. It is my nature to initiate and talk. It took me a long time to finally learn (and I'm still learning) that asking questions and listening is often more missionally powerful than giving a speech.

And why is that? Because Jesus is already up to something in people's lives. We need to let them tell us about it. It may come all at once or little by little over months. But if we listen and ask the next question, we will come away being a part of the kingdom coming and the will of the Father being done in their lives.

My favorite illustration of this insight is the story of an introvert who lives next door to a recluse. The introverted woman is a friend of ours who is determined to be a part of Jesus' mission.

These two women had been neighbors for 20 years, each married and raising their families. They had been friendly to each other but never friends. Then about ten years ago, so gradually that my introverted friend didn't realize it, the neighbor began withdrawing into her home.

They would see the husband out and about but not the wife. In time, her car had a cover over it – it never moved. The husband said that his wife was afraid to go outside or receive visitors.

Then a few years ago, the husband mentioned he was sick. My friend often told him to call if he needed help and his reply was always the same, "We'll be all right." She tried to keep up with how he was doing, and when she had not seen him or seen his truck move for a week last spring, my friend the introvert wrote them a note and taped it to their door once again offering their help and phone number.

Two weeks later my friend got a call. It was the recluse in a panic, "I think my husband is dead and I don't know what to do!" My friend ran over, calling 911 as she went. The recluse met my friend at the door. It was the first time my friend had seen her neighbor in years. The husband had apparently died while napping. My friend stayed with her reclusive neighbor throughout the ordeal of the EMT's, police, fire department and Justice of the Peace coming through the house and doing their jobs. She even let my friend take her to the funeral home twice, the last time to pick up her husband's ashes. The neighbor had said she was so thankful "you came to help me when I called." In spite of this relational breakthrough, or maybe because of it, the neighbor soon returned to her reclusive life.

So how does an introvert join the mission of Jesus in a recluse's life? Patiently and at Jesus' pace.

Today, the recluse still refuses any help and cannot summon the courage to come out or receive visitors. Nevertheless, through a series of notes taped to the neighbor's door, my friend has worked it out that she will call once a week to check on her. And that's what they do. The recluse will pick up the phone as soon as she sees it's my friend calling, but then tries to get off just as quickly. It's slow going. Brief conversations. Short notes from time to time. My friend has been able to talk with the recluse about God's love, which is hard for my friend to do as an introvert. However, the recluse has begun to receive this good news and has even begun talking more about how she feels ... lost and weary at this point.

My friend the introvert keeps offering to talk and to visit, uncomfortable as it is for her. But it's what Jesus is giving his introvert to do. It's going slowly, very slowly. But it is going ... at a recluse's pace. For Christmas, my friend gave her a devotional book. She wrapped it and stuck it in her neighbor's front door. My friend was afraid she might refuse it, but the neighbor called the next day and thanked her saying, "This might be just what I need." There is hope.

Patience. Space. Snippets of conversation that build on snippets of conversation over time. Jesus knew he needed a missional introvert to live next door to the recluse.

HERE'S THE POINT

The practice of talking with people happens in many ways. However, all of them boil down to this: Jesus can do more with two people who are talking with each other than he can with two people who are successfully ignoring each other. So, what kind of conversations are you having with the people around you?

CHAPTER 15
DOING GOOD

"Not all of us can do great things.
But we can do small things with great love."

—Mother Teresa

What if random acts of kindness aren't so random? What if the unplanned good we go around doing for people is actually planned out by God?

In fact, that's how it works. Ephesians 2:10 says, "For we are God's workmanship, created in Christ Jesus to do good works, which God *prepared in advance for us to do.*" (Emphasis mine.) A simple but important way to be in position to join Jesus on his redemptive mission is to be looking for people in our "neighborhoods" who are ready for a blessing. What good can we do for them? In fact, what good has God prepared in advance for us to do for them?

The fourth practice of doing good begins with us looking for the good we can do.

Sometimes we can plan to do something good in advance for people. But most of the time the good God has prepared in advance for us to do looks spontaneous and serendipitous to us. We weren't planning it, but we were looking for it. And so we recognized the opportunity when it arrived to bless someone with a word of hope, an act of kindness, an attitude of grace, a little time or a little help. The good God has prepared for us to do often seems small but will always be significant ... perhaps not to the human eye but to the redemptive plan of Jesus. Jesus speaks of little seeds through which God grows mighty works. Our job is not the mighty works; our job is the little seeds.

Mother Teresa once said, "Not all of us can do great things. But we can do small things with great love." Yes, this we can do because God has prepared it in advance for us. His work, our fun.

I appreciate the words of Clarissa Pinkola Estes – a poet, psychoanalyst, and post-trauma specialist — who wrote, "Ours is not the task of fixing the entire world all at once, but of stretching out to mend the part of the world that is within our reach. Any small thing that one soul can do to help another soul, to assist some portion of this poor suffering world, will help immensely." Well said. And as Jesus-followers it is our privilege and mission to watch for such opportunities every day. You just never know when it will be time.

By the way, in my experience when people begin to talk about doing good, they tend to think of doing good for random strangers along life's way. And, indeed, if you have the opportunity to bless a stranger along life's way, do it. However, what if we became more intentional and consistent about doing good for the people regularly within our reach? Our family, our neighbors, our co-workers, and so on. Think what would happen over time if once a day we planted a seed of kindness at our workplace. One seed every single day. How long would it be before we would see those seeds begin to sprout and bear their fruit?

"Not all of us can do great things. But we can do small things with great love."

Ironically, sometimes the good we can do is allowing people to do good for us. This may make some of us uncomfortable, but allowing people to bless and serve us in our time of need is also missionally powerful. It deepens the relationship. It blesses both the giver and the receiver. This is perhaps one of the hardest lessons for church worker families to learn. We are so used to giving and blessing and serving. We fight against being served and blessed. And yet sometimes this is the good God has prepared in advance for us to do ... letting our neighbor love and bless us.

There is another reason doing good is such an important missional practice. These days, at least in our U.S. culture, words mean very little. During the last political election cycle, how many of us believed all the speeches we heard or the promises made? When we drive to work and have the radio on, how many of us believe all the claims the advertisements make? We have come to understand that words are simply what people *want* us to believe is true rather than what is actually true. The fact is words have become empty to us. So it doesn't take much to understand why a non-Christian could dismiss our words even though our words are the words of God. They are categorizing our words with all the other words they hear.

Once again, some missional insight from Winnie-the-Pooh, "A little consideration, a little thought for others, makes all the difference." These days, because words mean so little in our culture, "a little consideration, a little thought for others, makes all the difference." Or to say it another way, it is important that people see Jesus in us before they hear about Jesus from us. The good works he has prepared in advance for us to do become the visible proof that Jesus is real. Words regain meaning because through our simple acts of kindness, people are seeing that the kingdom of God has come to them.

I have a pastor friend in Chicago. He has been trying to reach out in friendship to a neighbor. The neighbor knows my friend is a pastor and wants nothing to do with him. He doesn't want religion and figures that's what the pastor-neighbor is peddling. Then, one Saturday the neighbor unexpectedly shows up at the pastor's backdoor.

"Can we talk?"

"Sure. Come on in."

The neighbor sat down at the kitchen table and began to tell the pastor about what had happened the night before at a National Honor Society induction ceremony he had attended at the local high school. At the ceremony, he heard a speech given by a young lady who was being inducted into the NHS. It was a special occasion because this young lady is autistic. However, in spite of her challenges she had qualified for the NHS and had been invited to give the speech telling a little of her story. As it turned out, a good deal of her story revolved around Ben, who just happened to be the pastor's son. Ben was a student at the same high school. He was a senior and a big football player. A lineman. But every day Ben had made it a point to come up to this autistic young lady, get her attention, smile, and tell her good morning.

A simple act of goodness. Well within his reach on a daily basis.

What Ben couldn't have realized was the hope his simple act of goodness inspired in this young lady. You see, every day, Ben's simple act of kindness came in opposition to a bucketful of unkind acts and insults that made life at the high school very, very hard for this young autistic lady. In her speech, she said she often struggled in the morning just to summon the courage to face another day of school. But because of Ben and his simple act of goodness, she would find the courage she needed to face another day of classes. And tonight she wanted to thank Ben and let him know what a big difference his goodness had made to her. There wasn't a dry eye in the place.

And the neighbor wanted to come to the pastor-neighbor and let him know.

Somehow, this simple act of daily goodness shown to an autistic young lady not only blessed the young lady but slipped past the neighbor's shield he had built against religion. There was no baptism that Saturday morning in the pastor's home, but there was a new opportunity for conversation and friendship between two neighbors. All this because a young man took up the simple practice of doing good.

You just never know, but God does.

HERE'S THE POINT

The missional practice of doing good is the result of God preparing and us responding. What good can we do around here? How can we help make the kingdom and grace of God a little more real to people nearby?

CHAPTER 16
MINISTERING THROUGH PRAYER

"Thy kingdom come, thy will be done on earth as it is in heaven."

—Jesus' prayer in Matthew 6:10

You are terrified only once. Ministering to people by praying out loud with them may sound terrifying at first, but that's only because you haven't tried it yet. People who try it report that you will be terrified only the first time. If you can step out beyond your fear and find out what it's like to sense the kingdom coming near as you bless someone through prayer, you will suddenly realize it isn't so bad. In fact it's awesome!

Let me explain. When you have been seeking the kingdom, hearing from Jesus, talking with people and doing good, people will start to know who you are and know they can trust you. They will have found out you really do care about them. They will have found out you are approachable. That means it won't be unusual to have people stop and talk with you about what's going on in their lives. And when they share their burden with you, you will sense such a moment of transparency requires you to somehow respond. It would be weird to just walk away, correct? Their trust in sharing their burden with you requires some kind of response. In such a moment, what we often do is go with our default response, which is something like, "Wow. Well, good luck with that."

But, being missionaries, we can do better than that.

Instead of wishing them "luck" with their burden, we can help them with their burden. We can say something like, "Wow. That's a lot to be going through. Would you like me to pray with you about that?" I have been doing this for years and have found that when people share their difficulties, they are genuinely thankful to have someone offer to help them through prayer.

However, it gets better.

Next, after the person says yes to my offer of prayer, I then follow up with, "May I pray with you right now?" You see, people who say yes to prayer often assume that the praying will be done later, like during church or something. So while people may be thankful that you offered to pray for them, your follow-up invitation to pray in this moment moves them from mild gratitude to an actual encounter with the kingdom and the King.

And you will be terrified to do this only once.

You may be wondering, "Now, why do you consider praying with people a missional practice?" I have found a prayer spoken out loud on behalf of a person right to the King of the kingdom is a simple way to help them experience the reality of the kingdom being present.

On a practical note, I encourage you to keep the prayer simple. We can pray prayers that are involved and complicated. But if we keep it simple, we give the person a model of prayer they can imitate. They may be blessed by a prayer which has complicated language, but they probably won't be able to imitate it later. Also, when we are praying with someone, be careful not to address God as if he doesn't know what's going on or how to respond. I know I used to be guilty of this. I would feel the need to explain to God what a difficult situation we had on our hands and then basically give him instructions about how we wanted him to respond. Such a prayer can unintentionally leave a person set up to misunderstand their relationship with God. If an immediate positive answer is not forthcoming, they are left wondering whether God really wants to help them, rather than trusting him and relying on his presence, love and plan.

So instead of praying something like, "Dear Lord, my friend here has found out his wife has cancer," and then going into a list of all the things we need God to do for a satisfactory outcome, we can pray a shorter prayer that simply invites God into what we are facing. Something like, "Dear Jesus, you already know my friend here has found out his wife has cancer. We're scared. We invite you into our trouble. We ask you to heal her and help us to trust you as you work out your plan for her life. Amen." When we pray like this, we keep it simple and people feel blessed because they have invited God into their situation ... much like Jesus taught us to do with, "Thy kingdom come. Thy will be done."

Bottom line? When it comes to ministering through prayer, what matters most is not getting your words right but inviting your King in. By God's design, you are the physical contact point between your friend and the invisible kingdom which is present and available. Like we said, taking up the missional practice of praying with people may seem terrifying at first. But once we take courage and take Jesus at his word, we find out how missionally powerful this simple practice can be.

A friend of mine in Michigan sent me an email sharing what happened when she took up the missional practice of ministering through prayer: "Hey! I had the opportunity (and it's really a first for me!) to [take up the practice of missional prayer] with our lawn mowing guy! We were chatting and just before he left I told him to have a great weekend. He started to walk away and then turned around and told me that his mom, whom he is very close to, has cancer. She's in her 50's and has been getting worse. He had planned on going away for the weekend but now he was staying nearby in case something happened. Soooo ... I blurted out, 'Would you mind if I prayed for her?' I did and he cried and was so appreciative. I must say ... it was amazing to be a part of this! Since then, he seeks me out every time he comes over to mow and we pray. Unfortunately, his mom is getting worse and now has hospice care. But praying with him that first time certainly opened the door to ministering in a way I never expected."

Yep, you're terrified only once, then you find out how missionally powerful this kind of practice is.

And then there is my friend Wade from South Dakota. Wade is a former rodeo rider who, with his wife, participated in a Dwelling 1:14 training. As part of their follow-through on the training, they attended a block party in their neighborhood. Through the contacts they made that day they started developing friendships with people on the street. For the next several months they received invitations for BBQs, golf and more. These events were great fun but they also provided the opportunity for people to get to know Wade and his wife. Eventually people felt comfortable enough with them to ask questions about their faith.

I'll let Wade take the story from here: "On one occasion a man I was getting to know developed a tumor in his neck and was going in for surgery. I had already been calling him and praying for him during the biopsy and diagnosis of cancer, and he was a little shook about the upcoming surgery. I offered to meet him at the hospital on the morning of his surgery to pray with him and he was thankful I was willing to do that. The day before his surgery, however, I received a call from my sister in Omaha telling me my niece was hospitalized and not doing well. I felt I needed to go be with her. Knowing my friend's surgery was the next morning, and I had promised to be there for him, I decided to walk down the street to his house and tell him what was going on with my niece.

"When I got to his house, a group of four or five guys were sitting in the driveway having a beer. They offered me one and I sat down and visited a little before I told them what was going on. They were very understanding and I apologized to the one having the surgery that I couldn't be there the next morning. He was very gracious and said it was fine. But then I realized the opportunity that God seemed to be presenting, and suggested that we should pray for our friend right there in the driveway.

"Needless to say, I had several sets of blinking eyes looking at me, including the man I wanted to pray for. He was beginning to say yes but was still looking around at the other guys to see what they would think of it. At that moment the Spirit moved me to jump into action. I told the others to put their beers down and gather around our friend. I told them to put their hands on our friend and I began to pray. I was able to pray the love, care and healing power of Jesus into all their lives and gave thanks for the assurance that there isn't anywhere we can go that the risen Jesus isn't already with us. It was a simple, short prayer. But when I finished I looked up and some of the guys had tears in their eyes and one of them said, 'Wow, we have done a lot of stupid stuff on this street but we've never prayed for each other.'"

The beer drinking buddies may not have understood anything about the kingdom of God, but they knew they had encountered it. The kingdom had come and the will of the Father had been done right there on the driveway as it is in heaven. All it took was one friend who was willing to ask the missional question: do you mind if we pray right now?

Of course, there are other ways to take up the missional practice of ministering through prayer. Which of these might work for you?

- We can use our morning devotion time to pray for our neighbors using a Neighborhood Prayer Map (see an example in the Appendix at the end of the book)

- Every time we pray the Lord's Prayer we can be more intentional about inviting the kingdom to come and the will of the Father to be done in our neighborhood, workplace or school as it is in heaven

- Jesus tells us to ask the Father to send out workers into his harvest field (see Matthew 9:37)

- As we prepare for our daily mission trip, we can ask the Spirit of Jesus to show us what we need to see as we encounter people throughout the day (see Matthew 11:25-27)

- Every day, we can take the hand of our spouse and pray out loud for them as they join Jesus on his mission (we can do the same for our children)

- We can take our family for a prayer walk through the neighborhood

In the end, how we begin to take up the missional practice of prayer is not as important as simply starting. Remember, prayer is not so much about getting our words right as it is about inviting our King in. How can we help a person in prayer today?

So those are the 5 Practices: seeking the kingdom, hearing from Jesus, talking with people, doing good and ministering through prayer. As simple as they are, there is an underlying question that quickly emerges once we move from the "idea" of joining Jesus to actually living that way.

"Do I have time for this?"

My new friend Ray, from Corvallis, Oregon, put the question this way: "I live and work in the least churched county in the USA. I believe 'least churched' may also mean 'greatest opportunity to share the gospel.' The problem I am seeing is this: the economy is creating openings to share the gospel with hurting people like never before. However, many of the people who have the desire to reach out are running as fast as they can to keep their life and family above water. What is it going to look like for a lay person with a hectic life to have a missional life? If you can help me and other Christians figure this out, you might just see a tremendous harvest come in even the least churched county in the USA."

Did you hear what was behind Ray's question? The fields are ripe. I am ready. But I am "running as fast as I can to keep my life and family above water." How does a person with "a hectic life" have time to have a missional life, too? Layering one more thing on top of an already complicated life seems to put "joining Jesus' mission" out of reach for most of us. Correct?

But is that really what Jesus is asking of us?

As most people know, Jesus says in Matthew 28, "Therefore go and make disciples…" What you may or may not know is that the Greek participle that is most commonly translated as "go" in Matthew 28 is literally to be translated as "while going."

"While going, make disciples..." That changes a few things, doesn't it?

Jesus isn't saying, "go" as in "go find room in your hectic day to make disciples," but is rather saying, "while you are going through your hectic day make disciples." In fact, that is the answer to Ray's question. The key to joining Jesus' mission is realizing we don't have to find a way to come out of our hectic lifestyle in order to have a missional life. Our hectic life *is* our missional life. Jesus already has us where he wants us to be in mission. We don't have to struggle to add another layer of volunteer hours to our lives in order to "be missional." Our lives as they are now *are* missional... if we open our eyes to see.

It is "while we are going" through our normal hectic days that the kingdom of God is already showing us things. It is "while we are going" from appointment to appointment that the kingdom of God is already positioning us to notice people and talk with people. It is "while we are going" from the neighborhood, to the school, to the workplace, to the third place, that we take note of the opportunities already in front of us to do good and connect as human beings. It's *while* we are already going.

Over the years, I have occasionally kept track of how much time it actually takes me to respond to what the 5 Practices put me into position to notice during a day. Do you know how much time it usually takes me per day to respond to what Jesus shows me? Anywhere from a few minutes to about a half hour. Most days, I am able to respond to the opportunities Jesus places before me "while going." Responding literally takes no extra time because it is occurring as part of what is already happening. Sometimes, responding to an opportunity means stepping aside to have more of a conversation or stepping in to lend a hand, but those opportunities usually end up lasting minutes not hours. And the kingdom comes and the will of the Father is done.

So, each day, while you are running as fast as you can to keep your life and family above water put the 5 Practices into play and see what Jesus does. Seek what his kingdom is already showing you, listen for the words he's already speaking to you, talk with the people you're already meeting along the way, do good when it is within your reach to do so, and pray … for people and with people.

This is *how* we join Jesus' mission every day.

HERE'S THE POINT

The 5 Practices are effective at positioning us to enjoy people and to seek, recognize and respond to what Jesus is doing redemptively in their lives:

- Seeking the Kingdom
- Hearing from Jesus
- Talking with People
- Doing Good
- Ministering through Prayer

Next, with the 5 Practices in play, it's time to plan our first mission trip into the neighborhood.

CHAPTER 17
THE MISSIONAL PARTY

"So let's make the most of this beautiful day,
Since we're together, we might as well say,
Would you be mine? Could you be mine?
Won't you be my neighbor?"

—Theme song to "Mr. Roger's Neighborhood"

We drove the truck into the driveway, shifted into park, and we were there.

After living 18 years in the semi-rural community of Bullock Creek, Michigan, we had just arrived at our new home in the sprawl of Houston, Texas – the fourth largest city in the U.S. We got out of the truck, stretched and looked around. This was our new neighborhood.

The Mr. Roger's Neighborhood theme song started running through my head:

It's a beautiful day in this neighborhood,
A beautiful day for a neighbor,
Would you be mine?
Could you be mine?

I must have started singing it out loud because my daughter elbowed me and told me not to be so embarrassing. It didn't matter, because although we were surrounded by people's homes there were no people to hear me. The homes weren't abandoned. But the people who lived here had a habit that is shared by many in the U.S. Once a person arrives back in their neighborhood from a day at work or from a few minutes at the store, we park our vehicle and hustle back inside our home or apartment, right? Everyone knows that when we arrive home it's time to "cocoon" behind front doors and privacy fences.

So it wasn't really surprising, standing there in our new driveway, to look around at the homes in our neighborhood and not see neighbors. We knew they were in there somewhere. What was clear was that if we wanted to actually meet them, it would be a challenge. Of course, it would have been easy not to bother. After all, that is the U.S. norm. Live and let live, correct? Remember how we said 53% of Americans have almost no one to talk to? There are reasons for that. And one of the reasons is that we can live within 20 feet of other people, and it's normal not to get to know each other. Recently I read that 30% of Americans know *none* of their neighbors.

However, while that is the norm throughout the U.S., it wasn't going to be an option for the Finke family. Why? Because we knew we were called to be neighborhood missionaries. Acts 17:26 says, "... and God determined the times set for them and the exact places where they should live." The Finke's believe that. Proverbs 16:9 says, "In his heart a man plans his course, but the LORD determines his steps." We believe that, too.

So, while there were all kinds of factors that played into our deciding to live in this specific home in this specific neighborhood in this specific part of the city, in the end, we believed it was the Lord who had determined the exact place where we would now live. And for what purpose had he chosen this exact place? His purpose, of course:

to redeem and restore all people, including the people in our new neighborhood.

Believe it or not, God put you in your current neighborhood for the same purpose. You may have arrived in your neighborhood a few days ago or a few decades ago. Either way, it is not too late to join what Jesus is up to in your neighborhood starting today.

As we pointed out in chapter two, our "neighborhoods" are certainly not confined to the places we call home. God has put us in a variety of places where we are regularly within reach of the same people – work, school, places where we volunteer, play, etc. However, if we are going to learn how to join Jesus on his mission, our neighborhood is a logical place to start. Which brings us to the main question of this chapter: *How do we start?* How do we join what Jesus is doing in our neighbors' lives if we don't even know their names?

The Finkes' conclusion? Have a party.

We could have begun our missional adventure in a variety of ways. We could have gone from house to house knocking on doors and introducing ourselves as the new neighborhood missionaries. We could have launched a Bible study in our home, offering free gifts to anyone who would come. We could have regularly roamed the streets handing out religious pamphlets. Instead, we knew that if we could get to know people, Jesus was already taking care of advancing his own mission in their lives. We just needed to find out how and join him. So, the Finkes' job was simple: all we had to do was get to know and start to enjoy the people he had placed around us and then be in position (using the 5 Practices) to seek, recognize and respond to what he was up to in their lives.

So within several weeks of arriving in the neighborhood, it was clear that our first overt missional activity needed to be throwing a party. At least, it made perfect sense to us! Haven't you found that laughter plus the fruit of the Spirit make a pretty potent combination? Having said that, the goal wasn't so much about having a party as it was about creating an environment where people could meet, relax, have some fun, have some conversation and, over time, start becoming friends. In other words, our first overt missional activity would be creating an opportunity for our neighbors to meet and begin enjoying each other. In Dwelling 1:14 we now call this kind of opportunity a "neighboring environment."

"Neighboring" is defined as creating (or taking advantage of existing opportunities) which foster community and friendship between the "neighbors" where we live, work, play or go to school. Neighboring begins the process of awakening community in a neighborhood and friendship between neighbors. Whenever we create an environment where "neighboring" can happen, we call that a "neighboring environment."

Some might have trouble seeing a party as being missional. If "missional" is equated with something being overtly "religious," then I would agree that a party is not missional. However, if missional is about being with people and getting to know them so we can join whatever Jesus is doing, then, yes, a party can definitely be missional. The party (or any gathering of people) provides an environment or opportunity for us to get to know and start to enjoy the neighbors God has placed around us. As conversations turn into friendship, missional things start to happen – not because we force them but because friends trust each other. What acquaintances would hide from each other friends share with each other. We are long-term missionaries, not short-term evangelists. Short-term evangelism can be done without the context of friendship. But long-term life transformation (the redemptive and restorative mission of Jesus) happens most powerfully in the context of trusting friendship over time.

Here is a simple Neighboring Formula that illustrates how friendship emerges:

$$\frac{\dfrac{\text{Unhurried Time}}{\text{+ Proximity}}}{\dfrac{\text{+ Activity (usually involving food)}}{\dfrac{\text{Conversation}}{\text{x Over Time}}}}$$

FRIENDSHIP

Put people in an environment where they have unhurried time, proximity and an activity (which includes food) and you will see conversations emerge. Do this every once in a while over time and you will see friendships emerge. Do this with neighbors and you will see a neighborhood emerge. Since the 1950s, sociologists have known the three conditions necessary for fostering friendship: 1) proximity; 2) unhurried, informal interactions; and 3) a setting that encourages people to let their guard down and confide in each other.

Sounds like a neighboring environment to me!

Having said that, we might look at the Neighboring Formula's "unhurried time" requirement and think it's a deal breaker for us. Who has unhurried time? Allow me to clarify: unhurried time doesn't mean setting aside hours and hours with nothing to do. Unhurried time is a mindset and attitude we have when we are with people in a neighboring opportunity. We might only be able to be with a person 10 minutes, but it still can be unhurried time. Of course, the more unhurried time the better. Remember, hanging out was Jesus' inefficiently effective method for mission. Either way, by unhurried time we mean that when we are with a person we focus on the person. In other words, be where you are. Don't be in a hurry to get on with the next thing and miss the moment Jesus has presented you. Put aside all the extra things swirling around in your mind, take a deep breath, relax and be with the person. With that attitude and mindset even brief encounters can be deeply redemptive.

Unhurried neighboring, over time, allows us to begin answering our key missional questions about the people God has put around us:

1.   Who are these people?

2.   What is Jesus already up to in their lives?

3.   How can I join him?

Over time, as we enjoy getting to know our neighbors, we will find out who is far from God, who is ready for God, who are the church-goers *not* interested in mission, and who are the like-minded Jesus-followers who are ready.

By the way, as you are beginning this process in your neighborhood (or workplace, etc.) there is a simple way to discern who Jesus may have already prepared for you to meet. In Luke 10 Jesus is sending out the 72 to announce the arrival of the kingdom of God. Part of his instruction was, "When you enter a house, first say, 'Peace to this house.' If a *man of peace* (emphasis mine) is there, your peace will rest on him; if not, it will return to you. Stay in that house, eating and drinking whatever they give you …" (Luke 10:5-7). We can receive Jesus' instruction, as well. Look for "the person of peace." Who is the person who seems to be open to your good will and peace? Who seems to be open to talking with you? This may be the person of peace Jesus has been preparing to interact with you.

As you think about the people in your various "neighborhoods" (home, work, school, etc.), who may be your person of peace? Who, if you created the opportunity, might be open to becoming better friends? Take some time to pray about this and write down the names that come to you.

Remember the young couple from our missional community I told you about in chapter twelve? When they moved from their suburban apartment into one of the poorest parts of the city, they needed to answer the same missional questions we did, starting with "Who are the people around us?" In their new neighborhood, the answer to that question was that their most immediate neighbors were the drug dealers that hung out on the corners nearby. Did God want our friends to get to know the drug dealers? Apparently so. After all, once you take away the labels, they are young men who need the redemption and restoration of Jesus just like anyone else. Our friends didn't know how to get started, though. How do you get to know people who happen to be drug dealers? Throwing a block party didn't seem to be the right move.

As it turned out, it actually started with a wave.

As our friends would drive in and out of their neighborhood, they drove right past the drug dealers every time. At first, the drug dealers would think they were buyers driving in. You see, that was the only time these young men would see white people driving into their neighborhood. However, once they figured out our friends weren't going to buy drugs, it started getting a little awkward. Not dangerous, just awkward. So, Matt, one of our friends, started to wave as he drove by, just so it wouldn't be quite so awkward. Well, guess what? The drug dealers started waving back. Who knew drug dealers waved? After a while, just waving started feeling awkward, too. So one day Matt stopped, rolled down his window and said, "Hi. You know, I pass by here all the time. I'm Matt. What's your name?" So over time they all moved from awkward, to waving, to brief conversations.

One night during our missional community, we were talking about the redemptive conversations we were able to have during the week (missional practice #3, talking with people). I then introduced to them the possibility of the "person of peace." I asked, "Who might be a person of peace in your life right now?" Matt looked at his wife, Michelle, and they both said, "Big Larry." Big Larry was one of the dealers. Could Big Larry be a person of peace? Absolutely. If Jesus could work in the lives of tax collectors and sinners in the Gospels, why not in the lives of the neighborhood dealers? So we began praying for Big Larry, and Matt and Michelle started looking for opportunities to have more conversations with him. They tried inviting him to come to a meal in their home, but he said no. Then a few days later, Big Larry invited them to come to his aunt's home for a meal. Who knew drug dealers had aunts? But they do. They are people. And once we drop the labels, all of our neighbors are people who need the redemption and restoration Jesus offers.

That was Matt and Michelle's way to start neighboring: one person at a time. And, as I said earlier, our way was a block party. How did it go?

We teamed up with a neighbor we met across the street from our home and began to plan the party. Our plan was simple. We would invite the neighbors to come together for some good food and good times. We would get a smoker and provide BBQ for everyone (always a guaranteed hit with neighbors!) and we would ask the neighbors to bring a dish to pass and a chair to sit on. We made up fliers and decided to invite the people whose homes we drove by every day as we made our way out to the main drag of our neighborhood. That would be about 25 homes. We figured maybe half of them would actually come and that we would plan on having maybe 25 or 30 people tops.

85 showed up.

We didn't mean to have 85 people. It just happened. (Actually, God did it.) Most of the neighbors we invited decided to come after all, plus word had spread among neighbors just beyond our "invitation zone." Thankfully we had plenty of meat smoking! However, one thing was abundantly clear from the kind of turnout we had. People, whether they realized it or not, were hungry for community!

That evening, as people started arriving around 5:30 we could tell they were a little hesitant. Even though most of the people lived within 100 yards of each other they didn't really know each other ... yet. But as the food was served and people started sitting with each other eating and chatting, we saw the Neighborhood Formula (and the Holy Spirit) start to take over. Conversations emerged everywhere.

Unhurried time + proximity + activity (food) = conversation.

By 10:30 that night there were still people talking, laughing and getting to know each other. Friendship was emerging. A couple months after our first block party, we had a second – except my wife and I didn't have to organize this one. Other neighbors wanted in on the fun of organizing an event. Then another gathering was announced a few months after that one. These days, it is not unusual to have some kind of fun happening in our neighborhood every few months. Some gatherings are larger and others are much smaller. However, our original block party had catalyzed a simple but powerful shift in our neighborhood – we had moved from ignoring neighbors to enjoying neighbors.

What used to be a neighborhood full of strangers living on the same block has become a neighborhood full of friends. We have found people who are close to God and far from God. We have found like-minded missionaries and pharisaical church people. We have found several people of peace. And throughout the neighborhood, conversations have grown beyond small talk to meaningful sharing. There's lots of fun and laughter and kidding around, but there is also trust and transparency when life gets tougher. And in the midst of all this, it has become easier and easier to seek, recognize and respond to what Jesus is doing in the lives of the people we are enjoying.

There has been plenty of hanging out and having fun among neighbors over the last few years. But because of that there have also been a lot of spiritual conversations ... not because my wife or I forced them, but because it was what Jesus was up to in our neighbors' lives. We've listened as neighbors shared their difficulties and then we have had the opportunity to gently offer good news. We are careful not to pull out our Jesus-hoses. Instead we seek to offer a cool-cup-of-water of Jesus. Among the eight homes right around us, we have prayed at various times with all eight families. Most of them multiple times. This past Easter, 75 neighbors showed up at sunrise in an open lot next to our home to celebrate Jesus' resurrection. For about half of them, our neighborhood gathering was the only place they knew to come that Easter Sunday morning.

Why did we have 75 neighbors show up for an Easter Sunrise gathering this year? Because we threw a missional party with our neighbors that first year. We had come from being strangers to being friends. You see, once we have the fabric of friendship woven between us, you just never know what Jesus might do.

HERE'S THE POINT

Over time, neighboring allows us to answer key missional questions about the people God has put around us:

1. Who are these people?

2. What is Jesus already up to in their lives?

3. How can I join him?

CHAPTER 18
WHAT WILL YOUR STORY BE?

"Which of these three do you think was a neighbor to the man?"

—Jesus' question as he concluded the Good Samaritan

The expert in the law had asked a question meant to test Jesus. "And who is my neighbor?" The question ended up testing the expert in the law. In answer to his question, Jesus told the story we now know as the Good Samaritan. At the conclusion of the Good Samaritan, Jesus asked a question of his own, "Which of the three [a priest, a Levite or a Samaritan] do you think was a neighbor to the man?" It is a clever question because it puts the reader into the position of wanting to be a part of the right ending to the story. In other words, do I want my story to end like the priest's and the Levite's did? Obviously not. I don't want to be that person who is in too much of a hurry or too full of themselves to be a neighbor to someone in their path.

I want my story to be like the Samaritan's story. Jesus' response? "Go and do likewise."

My wife and I have the great fun of helping people, "Go and do likewise." Part of our Dwelling 1:14 missional trainings help people start to be good neighbors again. As a result, new stories are being told in neighborhoods across the country. There is the family in western Michigan who had lived in their neighborhood for six years without really knowing anyone. So they invited their neighbors to a cook out.

As folks were talking and getting to know each other they found two households who had lived a few houses from each other for 17 years and had never met! Talk about an important shift in the neighborhood. Another couple lives in a small apartment in New York City. There's simply no room for parties in their place. So instead of hosting gatherings, they go to gatherings others are hosting. In this way they are getting to know their neighbors and some of their neighbors' friends. A man who works in the Houston Medical Center started praying for the people in the "neighborhood" of his vanpool. He has slowly gotten to know several men and now hosts a weekly gathering in his home where each man brings a 22 ounce bottle of craft beer to sample. The conversations are becoming consistently deeper and more spiritual as the trust level grows. A husband in Oregon contracted leukemia. He and his wife spent long days and even weeks in Portland while he was receiving treatment. They couldn't even be in their neighborhood! But they began to see that they were in a new neighborhood – the neighborhood of the hospital. They began taking the time to meet and talk with the people who were also receiving treatment. Pretty soon the wife was leading a regular prayer time in the waiting area with anyone who was open to it.

What will your story be?

As you look out over the mission field of your own neighborhood, what is a simple, fun way for you to start neighboring? Maybe having a party is not for you. That's okay. Remember, the goal is not a party per se. It is creating opportunities for getting to know and starting to enjoy the neighbors God has put with you. That means there are any number of ways you can begin neighboring whether you're an introvert or extrovert, suburbanite or city dweller.

Below are several examples of neighboring that our family has enjoyed or that we have heard about from others. Neighboring Environments can be planned intentionally or happen spontaneously (that is, we can put ourselves into position to have spontaneous but meaningful encounters with neighbors). Which of the following might work for you? Put a mark by the ones which may be a fit.

Intentional Neighboring Environments:

1. Have a cook out or ice cream party and invite your neighbors.

2. Have a fire in the fire pit, provide the ingredients for s'mores, and invite your neighbors.

3. At work, look for someone who is regularly overlooked and underestimated. Invite them to lunch with you and one or two other employees.

4. Participate in gatherings hosted by others, like Home Owners Association functions or parties thrown by other neighbors. Go to community gatherings like festivals, art shows, and city celebrations. Be open to talking with people.

5. Give out baked goods to neighbors and be willing to linger if conversations begin.

6. Invite neighbors to a happy hour in your driveway.

7. Do a food-drive or invite your neighbors to join together and somehow make a difference for the community.

8. Invite neighbors or co-workers over to watch the big game.

9. Invite neighbors or co-workers to a wine or craft beer tasting party. Have everyone bring their favorite kind and share what they like about their choice.

10. Do you enjoy exercising ... or would you like to start? Invite neighbors to regularly power-walk or bike with you.

11. If your child is involved in a school group (like band, sports or drama), invite those families over for some fun.

12. Invite a different neighbor over for lunch or dinner once a month.

13. If you live near a university, see if they have a way for you to invite international students to your home.

14. What is your hobby or recreational sport? Invite others to join you.

15. Work with neighbors to have a community garage sale and give the money for a community cause.

16. Have an Easter Egg hunt with the neighborhood children and then use Resurrection Eggs (available at Christian Bookstores) to tell what really happened Easter morning.

17. In neighborhoods with multiple cultures represented, have a multi-cultural dinner with people bringing their favorite cultural dish.

18. At Christmas, make cookies for the neighbors and put a note on the plate inviting them to contact you if they need someone to take in their mail or collect the trash cans if they go out of town.

19. At home during the afternoons? Begin an after-school club for the neighborhood kids or have a regular story time for younger kids.

20. During the summer, hold a neighborhood VBS.

Spontaneous Neighboring:

1. Find reasons to be in your front yard rather than closed up in the house or apartment. Watering flowers, weeding, sitting on the front porch or driveway, etc. puts you into position to see who might wander by.

2. When you stop for your morning coffee, don't go through the drive-through. Stop and go inside. Be aware of the people around you. Look for people that just "happen" to be looking around as you are. Smile. Look for people who are regularly there when you are. Eventually introduce yourself.

3. Walk your dog when you see others are out walking theirs. There are few easier ways to meet people.

4. Be a regular at the neighborhood pool, community center or park.

5. Be quick to offer assistance to neighbors who need a hand with a project.

6. Offer to babysit for weary moms or so a young couple can have a date night.

7. Be a "regular" at a lunch spot. Start to get to know the wait staff and other "regulars." Tip well.

8. Let your kids play in a park-league. Strike up conversations with other parents.

9. Have a regular game-playing time out in the front yard with the neighborhood kids. Kickball, whiffle ball, basketball, touch football, tag, water balloon fights and more.

10. Bring morning treats to work. See what happens.

And what do we do before, during and after we start our missional work of neighboring and putting the 5 Practices into play? We take up the missional gift of prayer. Someone once said, "When we work, we work. But when we pray, God works." We highlighted prayer as we unpacked the 5 Practices in chapter sixteen. Let me now give you a simple prayer tool. Look for the copy of a Neighborhood Prayer Map in the Appendix at the end of the book. The Map gives you the opportunity to literally map out where your neighbors live, who they are and how you can help them in prayer. Take a moment to fill out your Neighborhood Prayer Map as well as you can. As you pray for your neighbors and have opportunities to meet and talk with them, you can add information to your Map.

What will your story be?

HERE'S THE POINT

How do we get to know the people with whom God has put us? Neighboring Environments: Unhurried time + proximity + activity (food) = conversation x over time = friendship. Jesus can do more with neighbors who are friends than he can with neighbors who are strangers. Begin planning your Neighboring Event today.

CHAPTER 19

WITH A LITTLE HELP FROM MY FRIENDS

"And let us consider how we may spur one another on toward love and good deeds. Let us not give up meeting together, as some are in the habit of doing, but let us encourage one another..."

—Hebrews 10:24-25

Imagine missionaries from all around Nepal, Ghana, or Indonesia coming together on a regular basis to share the stories of what they have seen God doing in their mission fields. Imagine them having the opportunity to share with each other what they are learning through trial and error – both what is working and what is not working. Imagine the support, insight and positive accountability the missionaries would receive gathering like this. Imagine how encouraged they would be; how inspired they would be to press ahead; how much better equipped they would be for going back to their corner of the kingdom and starting another stretch of mission-living.

With a little help from their friends, the missionaries would have their batteries recharged, their missional toolbox restocked and their hearts refilled. Of course, they are well aware that their mission is not fulfilled as they meet with the other missionaries. They know their mission can only be carried out in the mission field. However, they also know that without meeting regularly with the other missionaries, they could easily wear out and give up. So in that way, the gathering of missionaries is absolutely critical to the success of the mission.

Now imagine such missionary gatherings happening not just across a foreign country but across a local community. Imagine local missionaries coming together regularly from their neighborhoods, workplaces and schools for support, encouragement, insight and accountability. The exciting news is that these gatherings are happening across North America in increasing numbers! And you can be a part of one!

I call these gatherings of local missionaries "missional communities." There are many definitions in use these days for the term "missional community." If you Google the term "missional community," you can be overwhelmed! Each definition and expression of missional community may be legitimate in its own way. However, with so many definitions floating around, it can be confusing. So for the sake of us being on the same page, I define a missional community like this: A smaller group of people who gather regularly in order to support each other as they learn to seek, recognize and respond to what Jesus is doing around them every day as he carries out his redemptive mission.

When people start to see their daily lives as a mission trip and then participate in a missional community for support, insight and accountability, I see them quickly gaining insight and confidence in how to join Jesus. Right away they have stories to share of recognizing Jesus at work around them and joining him.

Every once in a while, when people hear me talking about missional communities, they think they hear me saying we should replace

Sunday worship with midweek missional community. Let me be clear, I advocate *both*. It is my observation that the congregations who have *both* vibrant Sunday worship *and* vibrant missional communities are the congregations seeing the most growth – spiritually, missionally, and numerically.

Throughout time, the rhythm of God's people has been to gather and then go, to come together for worship and Bible teaching and then go out for life and mission, to gather for Word and sacrament and then scatter into the harvest fields. Separating worship and Bible teaching from mission and Bible doing makes no more sense than separating eating and exercising. Eating without exercising makes a person fat. Exercising without eating makes a person starve. In the same way, I advocate *both* coming for worship *and* going for mission.

As we saw earlier, the key to joining Jesus on his mission every day is putting the 5 Practices into play. As we will see in this chapter, the key to staying intentional and inspired for this missional lifestyle is the missional community. It is easy to get busy and distracted from seeking the kingdom or get stuck and frustrated as we are neighboring. However – to steal a lyric from Ringo Starr – with a little help from our friends we can press through these times and continue the mission-adventure with Jesus.

Why is the missional community essential to our missionary lifestyle? It is not just the gathering, but why we gather and what we do while we are together. The *reason* we gather is specifically to support each other as we learn how to seek and respond to what Jesus is doing redemptively in the lives of people around us. The *way* we do this is through asking each other what I call the "5 Questions."

The 5 Questions are simply questions which correspond to the 5 Practices. When we gather in our missional community, the 5 Questions give each person the opportunity to tell their stories of what happened as they put the 5 Practices into play along life's way.

The 5 Practices with their corresponding 5 Questions are the following:

1. Seeking the kingdom: How did you see God at work this week?

2. Hearing from Jesus: What has Jesus been teaching you in his Word?

3. Talking with People: What kind of conversations are you having with pre-Christians? (By "pre-Christians" we mean to err on the side of hope!)

4. Doing Good: What good can we do around here?

5. Ministering through Prayer: How can we help you in prayer?

When missionary friends gather at our home for missional community, we take time to relax and reconnect, but then we can't wait to sit in a circle and start hearing and telling our God-stories! What I have learned over the years is that the key to people staying intentional and inspired for long-term missional living is the hearing and telling of our stories. The 5 Questions simply give us the launch pad for doing that. Here's the simple dynamic at work: Our mission-stories reinforce our mission-values, our mission-values reinforce our mission-practices, and our mission-practices ensure there are more mission-stories to tell.

In fact, at the end of Dwelling 1:14 trainings I usually sum up by saying, "If you only do one thing as a result of today's training, begin gathering with some friends and start asking each other the 5

Questions." Why? Because I know that when we start asking each other how we have seen God at work in our lives we will be much more intentional about looking. When we ask each other about what Jesus is teaching us in his Word we will be much more intentional about being in his Word. When we ask each other the 5 Questions we are gently but surely holding each other accountable to what we said we wanted to be putting into practice every day.

Likewise, when we hear each other tell our stories about how we saw God working last week, it inspires us to do the same. Not only are we inspired, we gain insights and tools for how to do it. When we hear each other's stories about talking with people, we recognize how close we have been to being able to have a similar story. When we hear each other's stories about struggling, we realize we're not the only ones who struggle and we can help each other re-engage the missional adventure.

Bottom line: Missional stories reinforce missional values, which reinforce missional practices, which produce more missional stories! On the other hand, if we stop gathering to tell our stories, our value for missional practices begins to fade. When our value for missional practices begins to fade, we no longer are as intentional about putting the missional practices into play. And when we are no longer doing that, we will no longer have many stories to tell.

As I coach missional communities, it is not unusual for a group to start strong, but then begin to fade after a season. The reasons for this are predictable:

1. They stop meeting regularly.

    When we stop meeting regularly, we stop receiving the support, encouragement, insight and accountability we need to stay on the adventure with Jesus.

2. The missional stories start to become general and redundant. When this happens it is usually because we have stopped being intentional about putting the 5 Practices into play in our daily lives. Practices lead to stories. No practices, no stories.

3. Even with the 5 Practices in play, it seems like not much is happening kingdom-wise.

    When this happens it is often because prayer has become less important in our group time. We have stopped praying for our "people of peace," for the harvest, and for the kingdom to come. It is important to start giving more time to prayer during our missional community gathering.

On the positive side, when we renew our focus on prayer, encourage and hold one another accountable to putting the 5 Practices into play and continue to meet together regularly, the passion for joining Jesus on his mission is restored. This recipe reflects what the writer to the Hebrews said so long ago, "And let us consider how we may spur one another on toward love and good deeds. Let us not give up meeting together, as some are in the habit of doing, but let us encourage one another ..." (Hebrews 10:24-25).

So, imagine neighborhood missionaries from all around your city block, subdivision or rural community coming together to share the stories of what you've seen God doing in your mission fields. Imagine having the opportunity to share with each other what you are learning through trial and error – both what is working and what is not working. Imagine the support, insight and positive accountability you would receive gathering like this and asking each other the 5 Questions. Imagine how encouraged you would be; how inspired you would be to press ahead; how much better equipped you would be for going back to your corner of the kingdom and starting another stretch of mission-living.

With a little help from your friends, you would have your batteries recharged, your missional toolbox restocked and your hearts refilled. Of course, you know your mission is not carried out as you meet with the other missionaries. Your mission is carried out in the places you live, work and play. However, you also know that without meeting regularly with these missionary friends, you could easily wear out and give up. So in that way, what we call the missional community is absolutely critical to the success of the mission.

Allow me to tell you a few stories of people who found this out.

Stephen is an accountant by training but a neighborhood missionary by passion. Stephen was part of one of our first missional communities. He is diligent and earnest by nature. He is somewhat introverted and idealistic. He is eager to serve and not afraid to work hard. He likes to think things out and see things go according to plan ... which means in the unpredictable world of neighborhood missions he can sometimes get pretty discouraged. Truth be told, if I had some of the neighbors he had I could get discouraged, too. Stephen describes them as "characters." And they are. Having said that, they are the characters God has placed in his proximity. So they may be characters, but they are Stephen's characters to know and love and serve redemptively with Jesus.

As I mentioned, Stephen was part of one of our first missional communities. Often he would come to the missional community on the verge of discouragement. He would be concerned about how things were or were not progressing with his neighbors spiritually. However, when we went through the 5 Questions and Stephen would tell his stories, to us who were listening, it sure sounded like great progress was being made! In fact, we would often be slack-jawed in amazement over how Jesus had positioned him to have a conversation with a neighbor. But Stephen usually wouldn't have seen the progress himself. He had the ultimate win in mind, that is, people confessing Jesus as Savior and being baptized into the faith. And because week after week he had no baptisms to report, he could get discouraged. The rest of us, of course, could see great progress being made. No, the ultimate goal had not yet happened, but many of the steps that could lead to that goal were happening each week!

Had Stephen not received this encouragement or heard our perspective on the progress he was making, he may have worn out and given up. Instead, each week as Stephen headed back to his mission field, he was encouraged, prayed for, and ready for the next steps of his mission-adventure. With a little help from his friends, Stephen stayed engaged in his neighborhood mission field rather than giving up.

Sam is an ex-Marine and a retired police officer who currently works for a private security company in Afghanistan. He looks the part, too. Shaved head, big muscles, and some pretty serious fire power in his hands when he is on the job. Sam is also a Jesus-follower, who, believe it or not, is pretty introverted. Sam and his family have been part of our missional community for a couple of years now; however, because of his job in Afghanistan he is only able to gather with us every once in a great while. You see, Sam works overseas for 105 days at a time and then he's home for 30. That means he's able to gather with his missional community maybe three or four times before he has to head back out of the country for 15 more weeks.

However, even though his interaction with the missional community was limited, it made a huge difference in how Sam was able to see missional opportunities and missional progress in his Afghan mission field. Sam's wife, Mindy, was the first person from their family to find out about our missional community and join our gatherings. She would tell Sam via Skype and Facebook about seeking the kingdom and joining Jesus on his mission. However, rather than getting excited, Sam got discouraged. While Sam had full faith that Jesus was present with him in Afghanistan, he just wasn't able to see how Jesus was at work in the men around him. And Sam certainly had no idea how to join him. The people Sam worked with were generally hard-shelled and very cynical about matters of faith and religion. Besides, like we said, Sam is pretty introverted. Given all these challenges, it seemed too difficult for Sam to be a missionary there.

Nevertheless, when Sam came home and joined us for his first missional community gathering, we started asking the 5 Questions as usual. Because of that, we were able to start sorting through what he was seeing among his teammates in Afghanistan. We helped him start to reinterpret what he was seeing as having Jesus in the middle. During the few times we were able to gather as a missional community, Sam had many insights from hearing our stories and being able to tell his own.

The question which still remained, however, was how would an introvert like Sam be able to take his conversations in Afghanistan to a more personal level? So, we began praying for Sam about that. ("How can we help you in prayer?")

The answer came in what seemed like an unlikely form. You see, Sam was learning how to tattoo. He had always enjoyed art and saw tattooing as a unique and intriguing form of it. When it was time for Sam to head back overseas, he brought his tattoo supplies along so he could keep practicing his skills while he was there. Pretty soon, some of his teammates in Afghanistan saw what he was doing with the tattoo equipment and asked him if he would be willing to tattoo them. Sam said he really was just practicing. But as it turned out, some of his teammates had the wrong lady's name on their arm, if you know what I mean, and needed someone to "fix" it. Skill level was secondary to being able to cover the old name with a new design. So Sam began practicing on real arms!

Tattooing someone takes a lot of time. It is not unusual for it to take two or more hours even for relatively simple tattoos. Do you know what Sam found out? During the time it takes to apply a tattoo, people – even hard-shelled security-personnel-types – tend to let their guard down and start talking freely with the person tattooing them. Sam would hardly say a word and men would start telling him their life stories and pouring out their hearts. So here was Sam, the introverted missionary, having meaningful and often spiritual conversations with men on his team without even trying.

It's what Jesus was doing.

The first Facebook message Sam sent me after returning to Afghanistan was the following: "Just wanted to say thanks to our group for all your prayers. In case you are wondering, Jesus is at work over here. I am still learning to keep my eyes open for what he is doing. I am so thankful for what he is doing in my life and in the lives of my teammates. As far as I can tell, there is only one other Jesus follower on my team, but I am having great God moments with the rest. Seeds are being planted for the kingdom. So, please pray for me that I would have the courage to surrender myself completely to what Jesus is doing. I am sure that a lot of this is due to your prayers and support. So, thanks! – Sam"

It wasn't too long before I received another Facebook message from Sam: "Hey Greg, Just wanted to let you and all of the others in our group know what God has been up to. Last night he showed up in a conversation with some of my team. It was crazy. One of the guys I had been tattooing straight out asked me if I was a Christian. I said, 'Yes, but ...' I explained how I was a Jesus follower and that the Jesus I know is the Jesus of the Gospels. I admitted that the Jesus of the Gospels was not necessarily the one that is portrayed in some of our churches today. I told them that Jesus didn't come to set up a system of rules like the Pharisees did. That he came to dwell among us and to forgive us, no matter who we are or what we have done. It was a long conversation, but when I was done talking about the Jesus I know, one of the guys who had been asking me questions got excited and said, 'Now that's a Jesus I can believe in!' It was awesome to have Jesus show up so unexpectedly. So, just know that Jesus is over here and his kingdom is alive and well. Please continue to pray for me and these men that I work with. – Sam"

With a little help from his friends, instead of Sam being missionally sidelined, he learned how to recognize and join what Jesus was doing in some pretty unlikely people. By the way, because of the tattooing, by the time Sam completed his next tour of 105 days he was known by all 200 members of his team and had had spiritual conversations with many of them.

Jason and Mary Ann were new to our missional community, underemployed, and struggling to make financial ends meet. However, perhaps as a result of that struggle, they were ready to rethink a lot of things in their life and learn how to look for what Jesus was doing in their life. When they came to the missional community, as usual, we used the 5 Questions to hear and tell our stories. By hearing our stories and telling their own they began to understand how to seek and follow Jesus every day. As they became more intentional and consistent in putting the 5 Practices into play in their lives, they had questions, but things were changing for the better. They were learning to put God first in every aspect of their lives. Each time we gathered, they would tell their stories of what Jesus seemed to be showing them and how they had responded. It was not always easy or fun. But as a result of re-centering their life on Jesus they had increasing peace and joy.

It wasn't long before they were able to notice how Jesus might be at work in their next door neighbor's life. Their neighbor's life was a mess but he was open to letting God bring redemption to his mess. Jason and Mary Ann began taking time to have conversations with him. They had him over for meals; and after several weeks, they came to our missional community with exciting news. Their neighbor wanted to be baptized and have his children baptized, too!

With a little help from their friends, instead of Jason and Mary Ann remaining spiritually underdeveloped and missionally unaware, they are now seeking, recognizing and responding to what Jesus is doing in their lives and the lives of their neighbors.

So do you want to be a part of a missional community? Do you want the encouragement, insight and accountability a missional community offers for joining Jesus? Then start one. You can do this! It is as simple as gathering a few interested friends and using the 5 Questions.

HERE'S THE POINT

While the 5 Practices put us into position to join Jesus on his mission every day, the missional community and the 5 Questions help us stay intentional and inspired for the missional life. Mission doesn't happen in our missional community, but mission doesn't last without our missional community. So, who will you invite? Where will you gather? When will you start?

See Appendix 1 for FAQ's on Missional Community

BENEDICTION

And now it is time to begin your new life as an everyday missionary.

No need to be nervous. No need to be afraid. This is what Jesus has been preparing you for.

Remember, you're not being sent out *for* him. You're being invited to come along *with* him.

And besides, you'll have a little help from your friends.

So, join Jesus on his redemptive mission, in the name of the Father who has been pleased to give you his kingdom, in the name of the Son who has risen from the dead and even now is on the loose in your community, and in the name of the Holy Spirit who has given you eyes to see and a heart to respond to the people Jesus has placed around you. Amen!

Now go have some fun!

DISCUSSION GUIDE:
JOINING JESUS ON HIS MISSION

"Lord, take me where you want me to go;
Let me meet who you want me to meet;
Tell me what you want me to say;
And keep me out of your way. Amen."

—The daily prayer of Father Mychal Judge, NYFD chaplain,
killed in the 9/11 attacks at the World Trade Center

SESSION 1: JESUS IS ON A MISSION (CHAPTERS 1-2)

Jesus is on a mission.

He has been sent by his Father on a grand adventure to redeem and restore human lives to his kingdom. Jesus is already on the loose out there in our neighborhoods, workplaces and schools. He is already doing the heavy lifting of working in the lives of every human being we see.

And he invites us to join him. "Come, follow me" (Mark 1:17).

Definitions: What we mean

- *"Missional Living"* is joining Jesus on his redemptive mission and living each day as if it were a mission trip into our own community. We are Neighborhood Missionaries.

- *"Missional Community"* is a smaller group of local neighborhood missionaries who gather regularly in order to support each other as we learn to join Jesus on his mission.

- *"Neighborhood"* is any network of people to which we have regular access. Who is regularly within our reach? Who are the people who live near us, work near us, play near us, etc.?

- *"Neighboring"* is any interaction that helps foster friendship between neighbors. Neighboring puts us into position to find out what Jesus is already up to in the lives of people near us.

1. The premise of the book is that Jesus is already on the loose in our community doing the heavy lifting of pursing his Father's mission in people's lives. All we have to do is join him. What intrigues you about thinking of mission and outreach in this way?

2. What was one "aha" moment you had as you read the first chapters?

3. How has Jesus been messing with you lately? What is he inviting you to notice, believe or wrestle with?

4. What did you learn about being an everyday missionary?

5. About which definition(s) do you still have questions?

6. What is Jesus inviting you to do as a result of today's discussion?

SESSION 2: MISSION MINDSET CHANGES (CHAPTERS 2-6)

Jesus is inviting me to join him on his mission.

This is an important mindset change for most U.S. church members. Jesus does not give me a mission to do *for* him. Jesus is on a mission and he invites me to come *with* him. I'm not a Jesus-*salesperson*. I'm a Jesus-*follower*.

The U.S. has become one of the largest mission fields on the planet. The river has moved. The odds are very good that right now, wherever you live in the U.S., the people in your neighborhood and workplace are largely unconnected to a local congregation and may not be connected to Jesus at all. We are no longer a church who is servicing a community filled with a variety of Christians. We are now a church who finds itself needing to be on mission in a mission field.

As Neighborhood Missionaries, we have a simple mindset:

In order to join Jesus on his mission all we really have to do is enjoy people and then seek, recognize and respond to what Jesus is already doing in the lives of the people we are enjoying.

1. Explain the difference between being a Jesus-salesperson and a Jesus-follower. What difference does this mindset change make for you?

2. What makes sense to you about the metaphor of the river moving?

3. What challenges do you (and your congregation) face now that the river has moved?

4. What gives you hope in spite of these challenges?

5. What surprised you about Jesus' secret missional weapon?

What do you think could keep you from imitating his strategy? How can Jesus help you overcome this?

6. What is Jesus inviting you to do as a result of today's discussion?

SESSION 3: SEEKING WHAT'S ALREADY HAPPENING
(CHAPTERS 7-10)

How do we seek, recognize and respond to what Jesus is already doing in the lives of the people we are enjoying? We start by paying attention to what he is already showing us. He says, "Open your eyes and look," for a reason.

We can summarize the theology at work this way:

- *The kingdom of God* (that is, the redemptive presence and activity of God in human lives) has come into the world to work out *the mission of God* (the redeeming and restoring of human lives to the kingdom of God) through *the people of God* (the redemptive presence and activity of God made tangible to other human beings).

1. What intrigues you about seeking what Jesus is already showing you?

2. What were some "aha" breakthroughs for you as you read the chapters on the kingdom of God?

3. Have you started to intentionally seek the kingdom of God in everyday life? How would you describe what you are looking for?

4. The kingdom comes to people from Jesus through us. How does this change the value you place in showing a little love, joy, truth or patience to the people around you? Tell the story

of an opportunity you had to do this in the last week.

5. What scares you about being an everyday missionary? What did you like about the analogy of the GPS and God's ability to recalculate when we blow an opportunity?

6. What is Jesus inviting you to do as a result of today's discussion?

"Can Jesus use imperfect missionaries?

That's all he ever does!"

SESSION 4: THE 5 MISSION PRACTICES (CHAPTERS 11-16)

As Neighborhood Missionaries, we have 5 simple mission practices we put into play as part of everyday life. The practices position us to enjoy people and seek, recognize and respond to what Jesus is already doing in the lives of the people we are enjoying:

1. **Seeking the kingdom:** The kingdom of God is the redemptive presence and activity of God on the move in the world around us. God asks us to seek it so we can find it. What are we looking for? We are looking for where God is showing us that grace can be applied. We are looking for where a little love and truth would make a difference. It often looks like human need.

2. **Hearing from Jesus:** Allow Jesus to continue discipling us and guiding us into his mission by opening one of the Gospels (Matthew, Mark, Luke or John) and joining the crowd following Jesus around. Listen to what he actually said. Watch what he actually did. Ask yourself, "What if Jesus means this? How does he want me to respond?" Hint: it usually begins with "humbling myself."

3. **Talking with People:** God can do more with two people talking with each other than he can with two people successfully ignoring each other. Talking with people means we do more listening than talking. We can do this randomly with strangers or regularly with people who live, work and play near us. This practice is for introverts and extroverts, honoring the relational pace with which God has wired us. Ask for the person's name, find out where they come from, and invite them to tell their story. Listen for what they are ready for. Take it one conversation at a time.

4. **Doing Good:** We are Jesus with skin on. When we find out what someone is ready for, we step in and help. What good can we do that will make Jesus' intangible love and goodness tangible to people around us? Remember, Jesus says he does his best work through the small things we do. Think "seed," "pinch of yeast" or "cool cup of water."

5. **Ministering through Prayer:** When trust has had time to build, people will start sharing what's really going on in their lives. When a person shares something real and hard, we can respond to them with a simple offer of grace: "Would you like me to pray with you about that?"

We put the 5 Practices into play every day as part of our missionary lifestyle. You just never know what Jesus may be up to!

Discussion: Go through each of the 5 Practices in turn and tell your stories of what you are learning as you begin putting them into play in everyday life (or share what you are struggling with).

Discussion: What is Jesus inviting you to do as a result of today's discussion?

"Starting is what stops most people."

SESSION 5: A MISSION TRIP TO OUR OWN NEIGHBORHOOD (CHAPTERS 17-18)

Being a Neighborhood Missionary begins with getting to know and starting to enjoy our neighbors. There are three simple missionary questions we can begin to answer:

1. Who are these people?

2. What is Jesus already up to in their lives?

3. How can I join him?

The best way to get to know and start to enjoy neighbors is to create a Neighboring Environment. In other words, we create an opportunity for neighbors to come together, hang out and allow conversation to emerge and, over time, friendship to blossom.

You can follow this simple Neighboring Formula:

> Unhurried Time
>
> + Proximity
>
> + Activity (usually involving food)
> _____
>
> Conversation
>
> x Over Time
> _____
>
> FRIENDSHIP

Several examples of both intentional and spontaneous neighboring are provided in chapter eighteen. Take a moment to review those. Which ones stood out as a good fit for you?

Have you filled out your Neighborhood Prayer Map (Appendix 2)?

Now you are ready to plan your first Neighboring Event. With one Neighboring Event, you can progress from *wanting* to be a missionary in your neighborhood to having *launched*. Take a few moments to fill in your plan below and then share it with your fellow neighborhood missionaries:

1. Pray daily using your Neighborhood Prayer Map

2. Choose one of the neighboring ideas from chapter eighteen (or choose one of your own making): My Neighboring Event will be _____

3. Who else might enjoy helping me?

4. Who will we invite?

5. What will be the date for the event? When will we have invitations out?

   Event date: _____

   Invite delivery date: _____

SESSION 6: MISSIONAL COMMUNITY (CHAPTER 19)

Neighborhood Missionaries need a little help from our friends.

The key to joining Jesus on his mission every day is putting the 5 Practices into play. The key to staying intentional and inspired for this missional lifestyle is the missional community. Those in the missional community help each other stay on the Jesus-adventure with encouragement, insights and accountability. The easiest thing for a Neighborhood Missionary to do is give up. It's easy to get busy and distracted or frustrated and discouraged. However, with a little help from our friends we can remain patient, press through these times and continue the mission with Jesus.

The way those in the missional community help each other with encouragement, insights and accountability is with the 5 Questions. *The 5 Questions are simply questions which correspond to the 5 Practices.* When we gather in our missional community, the 5 Questions give each person the opportunity to tell their stories of what happened as they put the 5 Practices into play along life's way.

The 5 Practices with their corresponding 5 Questions are the following:

1. Seeking the kingdom: How did you see God at work this week?

2. Hearing from Jesus: What has Jesus been teaching you in his Word?

3. Talking with People: What kind of conversations are you having with pre-Christians? (By "pre-Christians" we mean to err on the side of hope!)

4. Doing Good: What good can we do around here?

5. Ministering through Prayer: How can we help you in prayer?

When missionary friends gather in your home or at a coffeehouse or pub, take time to relax and reconnect, and then sit in a circle and start hearing and telling your mission-stories. The key to people staying intentional and inspired for long-term missional living is the hearing and telling of our stories. The 5 Questions simply give us the launch pad for doing that. *Telling our Kingdom-stories reinforces our Kingdom-*

values which reinforces our Kingdom-practices, which produces more Kingdom-stories.

Starting a missional community is as simple as gathering a few interested friends and using the 5 Questions.

Discussion: Each person choose one of the 5 Questions, and tell your Kingdom-story!

Discussion: What happened as your group heard and told their stories?

Discussion: What is Jesus inviting you to do as a result of today's discussion?

SESSION 7: FIRST THINGS FIRST

Joining Jesus' mission is not so much about changing the whole church as it is about changing our own mindset and practices and inviting a few friends to come with us. Think of a "pinch of yeast" as it gradually spreads through "the loaf" of our congregation. We don't try to convince the whole congregation to be "missional," all at once. We start with the few who are ready and willing to come along with us and put the mindset and practices of a Neighborhood Missionary into play as part of our everyday lives. Joining Jesus' mission is not about changing what we do when we go to church on Sunday mornings. It is about changing what we do when we go out as Church into our neighborhoods, workplaces and schools on Monday mornings.

1. What makes sense about the above paragraph?

2. Why focus on changing your own mindset and practices before trying to change anyone else's?

3. What do you most need God to change in you to become an everyday missionary?

4. How would you explain what an everyday missionary is to someone who has not read this book?

5. How would you explain what a missional community it to someone who has not read this book?

6. What is the mission statement of your church? How do missional communities help accomplish this mission? What if you choose to not have a missional community? What is likely to happen?

7. What is Jesus inviting you to do as a result of reading this book?

"Now that you know these things, you will be blessed if you do them."
Jesus in John 13:17

FAQ'S FOR MISSIONAL COMMUNITY

How many people should be in our missional community? There is no right number. However, we have found that it's helpful to start with a smaller number of people. A smaller number allows us to feel like we can experiment and discover for ourselves how all this works before inviting more people to participate. Also, a smaller number allows everyone to have adequate time to tell their story. As the group grows, it is a good practice to begin breaking the group into smaller groups during storytelling time.

Who should we invite to our missional community? Start with the few who are ready. While many may be interested, only a few will be ready to actually commit to living missionally and supporting each other in a missional community. And that's okay. Jesus loved and taught the crowds but only had a relatively few actually join him on the mission. We can follow his practice. Rather than trying to convince the unconvinced or accommodating those who are not ready to commit, we can start with the few who *are* ready.

Should we have husbands and wives meeting together or separately? While there is no right answer to this, Dwelling 1:14 encourages husbands and wives to participate together in the missional community whenever possible. However, if one spouse chooses not to participate, certainly welcome and support the one who does want to participate. Having said that, we have found that it is a real blessing for the couple when both of them participate and grow together in their missional life with Jesus. Plus, they are a natural example of the "team of two" Jesus sends out in Luke 10, "After this the Lord appointed seventy-two others and sent them out two by two ..." (Luke 10:1). While one or the other spouses may be more willing to take the lead, both are part of the team. For instance, I find it interesting how often God teams an extrovert with an introvert in marriage. A perfect personality pairing for missionary work! One starts the party and the other listens to the people.

How do we decide who should be invited to be a missional community leader? Missional community leaders may not be the type of leader you usually recruit to lead church programming. Rather than type-A, goal-oriented leaders, look for people who enjoy people and are good listeners. Often they will have the gift of hospitality or shepherding. In addition, I usually suggest the following attributes: someone who respects the pastor's leadership; someone who loves God *and* people; and someone who can follow-through on commitments. Missional community leaders are "initiators" and "facilitators." They take the initiative to remind people of the next gathering. They do more listening than talking. They ask follow-up questions to help a person come to clarity; and they help chatty people stay on subject and (when necessary) draw their story to a close. **Pastors:** when you are first introducing missional living to your congregation, it is our experience that no matter how badly you want to delegate the task, you are the best candidate to launch and lead the first missional community. Let your group help you. Let those who seem gifted and insightful speak into the process. But the congregation needs you to set the pattern. Having said that, give yourself and your group permission to experiment and figure things out. In time, because your group members have learned and discovered with you and through you, they will be ready to start a new missional community in their neighborhood.

Do we really use _only_ the 5 Questions? Nothing else? Don't we eventually need to move on to a more substantial curriculum? Dwelling 1:14 advocates using the 5 Questions as the core curriculum for the missional community. There are two main reasons for this. 1) Beyond salvation itself, there are few things more substantial in the Christian faith than recognizing and responding to what Jesus is doing around us. If we stop focusing on what the 5 Practices and 5 Questions prioritize, we will find our missional life shrinking back to what we had previously perceived. 2) It is our experience that if we allow groups to substitute studying a curriculum for asking and answering the 5 Questions, they will choose studying over accountability to missional living nearly every time. Finally, there may be an underlying question in play as well, "Won't we eventually get _bored_ if all we do is the 5 Questions?" Again, it is our experience that telling and hearing the stories of what Jesus is doing in and through our lives each time we meet never gets boring. The only time boredom starts to seep in is when members of the missional community stop seeking and responding to Jesus in their everyday life.

What's the difference between a traditional small group and a missional community? While the size of the groups may both be small, a small group tends to focus inwardly on each other and sees spiritual growth primarily as a result of studying and discussing. A small group tends to place its highest value on caring for each other. Of course, there's nothing wrong with such groups. However, a missional community focuses outwardly on the people in our various "neighborhoods." While we grow very close to each other and care for each other just like a small group may, our highest value as a group is to support each other as we figure out how to join Jesus on his mission every day. We see spiritual growth primarily as a result of taking what we believe and putting it into play via our missional practices the rest of the week.

We are used to using our midweek small group time as our time for Bible study. Do we study the Bible in the missional community? As you remember, question #2 is, "What has Jesus been teaching you in his Word?" The question, of course, corresponds to the missional practice of hearing from Jesus in his Word. The missional community champions studying the Bible, but is not the place where we study the Bible. Dwelling 1:14 advocates people being in worship and Bible study to hear qualified preaching and teaching of God's Word. The missional community, then, is not where we study more about the Bible, but where we report what we've discovered as we put the Bible into practice.

It seems to me the missional community would be a good place to invite people who are not yet Christians but are open to hearing more about Jesus and his teachings. Is that correct? Yes, this has been our experience. Think of it this way, what could be more helpful to someone trying to figure out what it means to follow Jesus than to be in a community of people doing that very thing! One of the missional community leaders I coach gave me an example of this. He told me about a young woman named Katie who started coming to their group. Katie is unsure of the Christian faith right now, but is open to investigating it. The leader told me Katie loves being a part of their missional community because she can participate so easily in the conversations launched by the 5 Questions and hear not only teachings *about* Christianity but stories of what happens when you *live* Christianity.

What have you found is the hardest part about starting a missional community? That's easy! For nearly everyone who is trying to launch a missional community, the hardest part by far is simply establishing the best time for your group to meet. Once you wrestle through that one, everything else is easy! Having said that, here's some help for getting through the process. As you try to negotiate your meeting time, realize most folks will find previous commitments getting in the way. Be ready for some to decide they can't be a part of the missional community because they "don't have time." This is normal. A friend of mine named Jay from Lombard, Illinois, coined a phrase when he was trying to schedule the launching of his new missional community. He found his own schedule stuffed full! That's when he said he was, "Over-committed and under-achieving." Yep. Join the club. However, don't give up and don't necessarily make attendance at the missional community a deal-breaker. Remember, the big deal is living missionally with Jesus every day, not just meeting as a missional community. It may take several months for people to conclude previous commitments before they can make new commitments to the missional community. So while people are working through this, work with them. Invite them to come to the group when they can. (Remember my friend, Sam in Afghanistan?) Keep them in the email/Facebook/Twitter loop. Even a limited participation in a missional community can make a big difference for people. But most importantly encourage them to begin putting the 5 Practices into play as best they can every day.

How frequently should our missional community meet? By way of answer, I would ask, "What kind of results are you expecting?" If you meet once a month, you should probably expect once-a-month results (which, as Sam proved, is a great improvement over never meeting at all). A best practice is for leaders to schedule the gatherings to be as frequent as possible even if some missional community members can't make every gathering. This keeps the schedule from becoming legalistic to people who can't be with you every time, and yet for those who can be there every time they benefit from the more frequent times together. Bottom line: better to have a person there sometimes than not at all. Finally, take into account the natural rhythms of your people's lives. There will be seasons when the usual schedule is not possible or preferable. Go with it. Because missional living is a lifestyle, taking off a week or more from meeting does no harm and may even refresh and rejuvenate the group for when they do come back together.

How should the first few gatherings go? Every gathering should allow people to relax and connect relationally. This can be done and still keep the group on track to conclude at the time upon which everyone agreed. The *first gathering* of your missional community could start with a simple statement reminding the people of why you are gathered. This actually is a best practice for *every* gathering. Something like, "We are here to support each other as we learn how to seek the kingdom and join Jesus on his mission every day." It is really easy to gather and start losing sight of *why* we are gathering. I repeat this kind of purpose statement at the beginning of nearly every missional community gathering. Next, using Question #1, spend some time letting people talk about what they have learned as they have begun looking for what Jesus is up to around them. You can also ask people to tell the group about the neighboring event they have planned. This can be a point of conversation over the next few weeks as people plan, execute and then reflect and follow-up on what God has done through their neighboring event. Finally, ask them question #5: How can we help you in prayer? The *second gathering* can follow the same general plan as the first. Remind them of the importance of putting the 5 Practices into play every day. Ask them how it is going. What is working and what is a struggle. Invite them to pick one of the 5 Questions and share their story. Then toward the end of the gathering, invite people during the next week to ask Jesus which Gospel he would like them to start reading. End with question #5. The *third gathering* can follow the same general plan as the first two. Be sure to ask the people which Gospel they will start reading this week. The *fourth gathering* can follow the same general plan, taking time to start unpacking one of the 5 Practices more thoroughly. Ask, "What are we learning about this missional practice?"

What should we expect the first few meetings that we might not think to expect? A few things are pretty predictable. *Expect* people at first to behave like they are in a church meeting rather than a gathering of friends. For that reason, I would encourage you *not* to meet at church. Meet in someone's home or at a coffee house or pub. Treat the gathering more like a party of friends than a meeting of church members. Many missional communities center their gatherings around a meal because they find it fosters more natural conversations. *Expect* not to have every person respond to every one of the 5 Questions. There are two main reasons for this: first, there won't be enough time; and, second, it will take some weeks for your people to figure out what the 5 Practices really are and how to put them into play in their lives. The purpose of asking the 5 Questions is simply to set up the opportunity for people to sort through and tell their God-stories and gain clarity as to how they might respond to what God is showing them. Getting through all the Questions is not the point. Telling our stories is. *Expect* silence from the group early on. But don't be afraid of it. Give your group room to think, process and come up with the words they need to express their thoughts or their questions. Think of this as unhurried time and be patient with the silence. Expect to learn as much or more from stories of failure and missed opportunities as you do from stories of things going well. Encourage people to tell their stories of both kinds. *Expect* people to be nervous at first about putting the 5 Practices into play in their daily life, or simply to forget to do so. Be persistent but patient in coaching and coaxing people to give the missional practices a try. At the same time, remember it takes a while to establish mission practices as natural habits. So be patient as they are gaining traction and momentum. *Expect* to celebrate a lot of baby steps. Baby steps are how we learn how the missional practices work and how we gain confidence. Leaders, be sure to tell the group about your baby steps. Early on, I made the mistake of telling the group only my really cool God-stories. Pretty soon I realized I was amazing them with my stories, but I was really helping them learn the 5 Practices when I told them about my baby steps. Besides, baby steps are *huge* compared to no steps. *Expect* to encounter frequent roadblocks to missional progress, especially in the early days. The evil one will try to thwart you. Instead of remaining stuck or starting to noodle through a possible solution on your own, stop and as a group invite God into the problem. Ask him to help you see what he is showing you.

How should we handle our prayer time as a missional community?
A best practice is *not* to have the leader take all the requests and pray for everyone. Instead, have each person turn to the person next to them and ask Question #5, "How can I help you in prayer." Then each person takes their turn praying. Couples can pray for couples. Be patient but persistent that each person says at least the briefest of prayers for the next person. Why? Because this is a safe environment for every

participant to learn how to pray out loud for people, which is a simple but powerful missional tool.

What is one of the best follow-up questions we can ask each other after telling our mission-stories? After someone has shared what they think Jesus is showing them or teaching them, or after they have told about a conversation they had or something good they have been able to be a part of, an important follow-up question is, "What do you think Jesus wants you to do now?" We ask the question simply to help the person gain clarity from Jesus and to take ownership of what they think he is giving them to do next.

Neighborhood Prayer Map

Instructions:
1. Draw a map of the streets and homes around yours
2. If you know the occupants, write their names beside their home
3. If you don't know the occupants write "?"
4. As you get to know your neighbors better, write additional details you can include in prayer.

Example:

ABOUT THE AUTHOR

R ev. Greg and Susan Finke are
the founders of Dwelling 1:14,
a non-profit ministry which seeks
to help Jesus-followers connect in
their neighborhoods, workplaces
and schools for discipling and
missional living (www.dwelling114.org). The name Dwelling 1:14
references John 1:14 and the incarnational, missional nature both
of Jesus and those who would follow him into the world. As Eugene
Peterson paraphrases in The Message, "The Word became flesh and
blood and moved into the neighborhood."

Greg and Susan offer coaching, consulting, and training experiences
for congregations and their leaders for discipling, living missionally
and multiplying missional communities.

Before founding Dwelling 1:14, Greg had been the senior pastor
of Messiah Lutheran in Midland, Michigan for 18 years and Gloria
Dei Lutheran in Houston, Texas, for three years. Susan has extensive
experience as a staff leader in children's and family ministries and
in leadership development. Greg and Susan have three daughters:
Amanda and her husband Kevin, Emilie, and Ellen. Greg and Susan
enjoy life as neighborhood missionaries in League City, Texas.

For information on ordering e-book copies
of *Joining Jesus on His Mission*, go to:

www.TenthPowerPublishing.com